Contents

Editorial

Welcome to the spoken word issue. Never underestimate the power of the spoken word. In a recent study, 'Yemen's al-Qaida and Poetry as a Weapon of Jihad', the academic Elisabeth Kendall found that poetry may be a powerful tool in recruiting new militant Islamic jihadists to that cause, due to the "power of poetry to move Arab listeners and readers emotionally, to infiltrate the psyche and to create an aura of tradition, authenticity and legitimacy around the ideologies it enshrines".

This raises certain interesting questions, is there something about the Arabic language that gives its poetry such reach and compelling power to speak to disaffected young men and women? What is it about poetry in English and other European languages that has seen it move in a century from perhaps the most central to certainly the most marginal major art form? Why, in this country does poetry seem so opaque, so unable to communicate collective consciousness or convey political messages to the marginalised in society? Some of this is to do with singularity of message. The dominant discourse in Wahhabism preaches a common narrative, without much room for nuance. Self-reflexive it isn't. More important, however, is the possession of a rebel voice or some indefinable cool factor. It is not just the jihadists that have their poetry, the Naxalites and nationalists are at it too. The poetry that Kendall is talking about is the Ginsberg or Ice Cube of militant Islam, presumably without the respective homosexual context or profanity, but no doubt with infidel crusaders taking the place of the LAPD.

Surely Arabic poetry has its high and low forms too? When one looks at this in a Western context, it is tempting to argue not every Arabic speaker is intimately familiar with the Mu'rabbah tradition or reciting Nabati oral poetry on their way to work any more than an average English speaker can quote passages of Chaucer or Shakespeare or remember Shelley's odes?

But there, one would very probably be wrong. Far from some essence in Arabic verse making it a recruiting sergeant for extremists, what Kendall's research slightly underplays is that it is the absolute centrality of poetry in Arabic culture that makes it a natural propaganda vehicle for extremists, rather than any special characteristic of the extremist poetry itself. To further the comparison, observe how reality TV performance shows like 'Prince of Poets' and 'Millions Poet' both draw massive audiences in the Gulf region.

So, is spoken verse finished as a means of cultural and political communication in English? Hell no. One only needs to look at Hip Hop to see that there is something there. Though you might argue that the fierce class and race politics of Gil Scott Heron and Chuck D have given way – more fully than the Feds could have hoped – to depiction of a flashy aspirational lifestyle.

But there is more to rap than Tinie Tempah's *GQ* fashion shoots. Bands like Hector

Bizerk and Stanley Odd – whose MC Dave Hook is featured in this issue – are making vibrations in the Scottish musical underground in ways that no fey indie act has done in years. It appears that Scottish audiences may finally be getting over the cringe factor about how their spoken voices sound. In fact, our guttural vowels suit the medium perfectly. To that end we present an interview with Scottish rapper and commentator Loki, aka Darren McGarvey, who talks frailty and power and how he sees his writing as a way to challenge both, exploring those voices excluded by the establishments of language, poetry, and politics.

And if that wasn't evidence enough, then surely the omni-stooshie that's been stirred up by Liz Lochhead reaching the end of her term as Makar must be proof that poetry is part of public and political Scotland. We'd like to thank Liz for the huge labour she put in to being Makar and the brilliant poetry and trouble she kicked up in the process. Her successor has not yet been announced as we go to print, but our votes would be for Tom Leonard or John Glenday. Though we'd be delighted too to have a Polish, Urdu, or Gaelic Makar, now that we've got English and Scots out the way.

But back to the matter at hand: call it what you will, the Scottish performance poetry/spoken word scene is thriving with nights like Neu Reekie, Inn Deep, Rally and Broad, Fail Better and countless others making it hard to go out these days and not be subjected to some poetry. We wanted to represent a little of that in this issue of *Gutter*. So we have work here from Aidan Moffat, Nick-e Melville, MacGillivray, Calum Rodger, Kate Tough, and Julia Taudevin. Conscious that performed work can't always be represented in full on paper, your loving and considerate editors have also prepared some mp3 files for your aural delectation. These can be downloaded for free at the *Gutter* website.

Its not all hip-hip-hippity-hop in this issue's poetry though. We have some good-old-fashioned ink-on-paper delights for you too. Amongst others, there's new poetry from Andrew F Giles, Colin Herd, Hugh McMillan and Patricia Ace (welcome back all, it's been a while), Jamie Norman's wonderfully political porcine picture poem (page 007), and debut appearances in the magazine from Andrew Blair, Alison Whittenberg, Leyla Josephine and Judith Kahl to name a few.

Some writers transcend the oral and the written forms in both poetry and prose. Jim Ferguson is one of those writers and we are delighted to include his brilliant short story 'Walmart Pants' (page 019). Read it out loud to yourself or a friend, or for a whole new experience go to our website and hear Jim read it.

There is more excellent writing about apartheid South Africa from Lynnda Wardle. We are looking forward to seeing these stories published in book form some day soon (Freight Books, are you listening?) Other prose highlights include Donald S Murray's 'I Dream of Mikhail Gorbachev', an extract from ES Thomson's forthcoming novel *Beloved Poison*, and two pieces from writers entirely new to *Gutter*: Marek O'Lasce and Stuart Johnstone.

It was with almost unbearable disbelief and profound sadness that on 22nd November 2015 we learned of the death of our friend and former Guest Editor, Alexander Hutchison – better known as Sandy. A supporter of this magazine from its inception, Sandy was a poet, translator, mentor, and above all a human being of great kindness, humour, spirit and generosity. His work and words touched a great many readers and writers across the world.

It is perhaps most tragic that not long before his death he was enjoying a late flourish of acclaim: his collection *Bones & Breath* having won the 2014 Saltire Award for Scottish Poetry Book of the Year. There is the obvious sadness of unfinished business, but tempered with great gratitude for what Sandy gifted us during his life. His most recent collection *Gavia Stellata* (2015) was a translation of his best-known work into Spanish. We are honoured to reprint three poems in this issue, alongside the Spanish translations by Juana Adcock. We are grateful to Hazel Frew for curating tributes from some writers who knew Sandy best. Turn to pp 087–103 to remember a fine life lived to the fullest.

this beer

Andrew Blair

Is for punks[1],
Candlelight
And battering rams.
Provokes,
Uses
Reaction as traction.
Is for Laika,
Bars and Lisichka,
Pchyolka and Mushka.
Works
It baby.
Marie Curie
Is full of it.
Whispering content at the edge of hearing.
Widespread, at a loss.
The dinosaurs.

---

1 Punk is dead[2]

Mistaken for its cyclical echoes/ Decomposing/

Fuelling/ An underground foundation/

Punk is dead/ And so buried/ Is infiltrated/

Rainwater rushes/ Its underground roots

Then returns to them from sky and/ Supermarket/ Spiralling into control/

We name this imbued downpour/ For its ancestors/

The wheel turns for everyone/

Is drowning/

Soon we will all be punk

2 Obviously

The Right Thing

nick-e melville

David Cameron tells ITV News he will take a 10% pay rise   saying
the right thing to do is to be paid the rate for the job

personally   the right thing to do is to be paid the rate for the job
but added
he didn't agree with IPSA's decision

The Prime Minister did not say what he would do
with his pay rise   but did say that
it gives you the opportunity to do more
in terms of charitable giving and things like that

We believe in standing up and helping   those people
who want to do the right thing   not the wrong thing

Next to doing the right thing   the most important thing
is to let people know   you are doing the right thing

You can always count on Americans
to do the right thing   after
            they've tried everything else

Sometimes it is better to lose
and do the right thing
than to win and do the wrong thing

If I lose the ball   I lose it   trying to do the right thing
That's the way it is

I truly believe we're on the brink of something special
in our country
we can make Britain a place   where a good life   is in reach
for everyone
who is willing to work and do the right thing

David Cameron has said it was the right thing to do
to give the troubled charity Kids Company a £3 million grant
just days before it was forced to close

Where Labour do the right thing   like those education reforms
we'll back them

A country that backs those that work hard and do the right thing

This is a one nation Government
that does the best thing for the economy
and the right thing for the country

to encourage people to behave responsibly
because they know that doing the right thing
and taking responsibility
will be recognised and will make a difference
post-bureaucratic politics is
about understanding that you can make
doing the right thing
more appealing
                    through incentives like money
You can make it easier for people to do the right thing
by removing obstacles or hassles from their path

apply gentle social pressure
by making it clear to people that others
        their friends and neighbours
are already doing the right thing

Responsibility is people   doing the right thing
That's not theory – it's fact

you are rewarded for working hard and doing the right thing

we have put our country back on the right track
Britain
is on the right path

Our goal is a country
that not only rewards those who work hard
and do the right thing
but gives everyone
        no matter their background
the chance to fulfil their potential

if you did the right thing
you were penalised
if you did the wrong thing
you were rewarded

with the unfairness of it all infuriating hardworking people

We believe that cutting people's taxes is the right thing to do
to provide the right incentives for people to work

That ambition remains the right one

it should be a right
for everyone

We are putting things right

the British Bill of Rights   and we will ban the police

we will introduce a new law
that will pardon those people
and right these wrongs

extending the Right   we have reinvigorated
the Right   right   across our country

We will extend the Right
We will extend the Right

It is unfair that they should miss out
on a right

under the extended Right
we will take forward a new Right
scrap   the Human Right

and the rights of victims
key rights for victims
including the right to make a personal

The Government will scrap the Human Rights Act
and introduce a British Bill of Rights

If you have worked hard during your life
saved   paid your taxes
and done the right thing

We are building a Britain
where everyone
who has worked hard
and done the right thing
can enjoy security   in retirement

to keep our family
of nations together   was right
the right thing to do
and the question of Scotland's place
in the United Kingdom is now settled

a British Bill of Rights will restore common sense
and lead the world
in promoting women's rights

the right of Israel
to protect its security
will continue
to support universal human rights

We will ensure our Armed Forces overseas are not subject
to persistent human rights claims

Tackling global poverty is both the right thing to do and in Britain's interests
Those who work hard and do the right thing must be rewarded
who do the right thing
working hard and doing the right thing

we will extend the Right

Prime Meats

Jamie Norman

PR 48 Leith Suicide. CP 32 KP <1 Hackney Suicide with Child. EJ 47 Sneinton Suicide. MR 36 Norwich Suicide. MB 66 Newham Suicide. MW 44 Bampton Starvation. SB 53 Solihull Suicide. EC 57 Holderness Drain Suicide. RC 62 Husband of EC, Depression, Death by Natural Causes? PW 33 Pignal's Enclosure Suicide. MWJ 26 Tregaron Suicide. DC 59 Stevenage Starvation and Diabetic Ketoacidosis. EL 53 Battersea Attempted Suicide. LR 39 Sussex Suicide. MM 48 HM 59 Warwickshire Suicide Pact. AL 31 Newark Suicide. LM 57 Stanley Park Overdose. LC 30 River Wear Suicide. RS 44 Southfields Suicide. NPB 51 Helmsley Suicide. TD 50 Sunderland Suicide. TM 48 Glasgow Pneumonia. MS 46 Southport Pneumonia. JK 39 Kingsthorpe Suicide. ET 39 Livingstone Brain Tumour. MO'S 60 London Suicide BM 34 Nelson Lancashire Suicide. TS 53 Staffordshire Suicide. MC 60 GH 55 Lincolnshire Suicide. MH 20 Manchester Suicide. Hendon Overdose. TS 53 Kinver Suicide. VH 21 Lancashire Suicide. CP 42 Ennerdale Suicide. DB 28 Firth of Forth Suicide. SC 55 Glendare Road Suicide. CB 21 Barry Suicide. JW 57 Wigan Suicide.

DG 56 Staveley Heart Attack. FP 58 Beighton Suicide. The DWP does not hold information on the reason for death; therefore no causal effect between the benefit and the number of people who died should be assumed from these figures.

But we were outraged by the pig.

Separation

RA Davis

a friend of mine,

Ben

met President Obama

a friend   of a friend of mine

Tom

was shot by a sniper in Gaza

a comrade   of a friend   of a friend of mine
I don't know his name

executed Osama Bin Laden

a sister   of a friend   of a friend   of my brother
she

was killed in a shooting in a shopping mall
in Toronto

a friend   of a friend   of a friend   of a friend   of a friend of mine

went to school in Dunblane

a friend   of a friend   of a friend   of a friend   of a friend   of a friend
of mine

is reading in the good light of an autumn afternoon in the café in the corner of the
square

Shut Out the Noise

Marjorie Lotfi Gill

– President Obama implores US lawmakers to 'shut out the noise'
and ratify the Iran nuclear deal

Close your eyes, cup your palms
over your ears, then speak. Say
the day they shot all the doctors
at the hospital for refusing to hide
bodies, I was the girl watching
from her grandmother's rooftop.
Say *the staccato of sniper fire*
was a call to prayer,
and the nightly track of tanks
a low toll of bell, more pressure
of sound than sound itself. Say
the fire at our school was set. Say
the man dressed in white robes
walking our blacked-out road
after curfew asked the question
without opening his mouth. Say
the words on every brick hurtled
through our window:
Yankee go home.

Interview Questions for God

Andrew Blair

— What was it made you want to tell this story?

— Why tell it now?

— How do you feel about being defined by your job?

— Is it lonely, sometimes?

— It's one hell of a cast, isn't it? Were you tempted to give everyone equal amounts of screentime or did you just not bother?

— Would you agree that some of the more interesting aspects have been watered down or glossed over in the editing suite?

— Do you feel that maybe you went overboard on the symbolism?

— How did you achieve free will? Was it done with practical effects or CGI?

— Some critics have mentioned the running time: were you tempted to end things a little earlier?

— You've had some pretty controversial stuff attributed to you, do you feel you were misquoted?

— Your PR team have been very keen to stress that you are a perfect, all powerful being who therefore could not fail to exist. Do you feel this puts unnecessary pressure on you in any way?

— Have you done a lot of interviews today?

— Do you ever get tired of hearing the same questions?

— Ever tempted to jack it all in?

— Do you need help?

— Would you ask for help if you did?

— Do you have someone to talk to when things go wrong?

— What's your favourite Jason Statham film?

Mommy, Daddy, You and I

Martin Law

1. Watch Television together.
2. Make kid simply informed by simply talking at them on the current political scenario. Make kid explore interesting cartoons on politics. Make kid know about the news piece.
3. Kid not worry: politicians are friend to each other.
4. Make kid know politicians make a History.
5. Do not criticize or make weird comments showing your mind. Talk on the parties and what the present country needs. Talk about administration that begins with home leading to countries. How do leaders manage and what it means for the nation.
6. Don't make kid overwhelmed during Election. Television, newspapers or people speak Politics and talk of parties. Kid get overwhelmed and anxious to happenings around. Take a break. Switch off the continuous bombarding of politics.
7. Kid can be anxious, who is best politician? Who gets the prize? Well, in our town, ask kid and he's blank on such political scenario. Parent's views do matter in this domain. They know about politics and they can influence and have lasting effect as kid grow. Childhood innocence do not last long as kid grow to learn values and make their own choice and decisions.
8. Lastly, make a kid to be absorb. Kid be informed voters in time to come when they grow up and be responsible, powerful leaders in their life – be in profession of politics, why not?

Remember, it is values to imbibe and hope brings in rays of sunshine. And kid can make a history.

A Device

Georgi Gill

may be planted under the stairs
in your grandmother's house,
behind Tesco's glass recycling bins,
beneath your boss's plush new Audi
(with genuine leather upholstery),
up river from a Japanese nuclear power plant,
in the silver bulb of the ceremonial mace
ahead of the state opening of parliament,
downwind of refugees waiting for chances
at Calais's Camp Jungle,
above the clouds at 36,000 feet
over the Atlantic Ocean in a Boeing 757,
in front of a dark eyed toddler (who may
or may not think it's a toy),
inside your mind.

Seven Stones*

Alice S Yousef

Skip the stench of the valley's moss
fiddling we will find the seven stones,
for the pillars of the future, the same we build and destroy,
to rebuild and watch the stones fall for fun, how cruel.

Fiddling near the roots of the yew
you call on to me. My hair, boyish to the sound of fury tangles
in the branches, as I split two snails from a molten brick,
knives, these fingers are. The brick is in my hand but you have the corner stone.

Skip the toads that croak in the pit, one we call the eye of the mountain
juggling oranges with a stolen fragrance we fiddle with hallowed turtles and sticks
children of drones, roam the valley for the seven stones
one atop the other, like pickles in a jar

for the perfect cut to finish the making of a pillar,
strong we rummage for the smoothest stone
digging the cracks of white sand, an early afternoon
in the shades of the milky almond

we meet a scorpion, venomous
you run towards me hurling poison onto the stone
Here, I give you a broken toothed rock,
one I searched the years for, in the grit that lines the valleys

on the roads I take alone
leaving the olives that dust the mountain and you to find the seventh stone
Pillars have risen, others from more basic material
lime and stone, iron and mud are other options for the heights of Babylon

Skip the stench of the seven stones,
the pillar is made for our bones.
Forget the crack as the stones we collect slide,
we will build and rebuild and the city, ours,
falls into cinder overnight.

---

* Seven Stones is a children's game, not unlike cricket or dodgeball, played in many parts of the Middle East. In the game, seven stones are piled on top of one another and one team tries to knock them down while the other defends and rebuilds. It is a game of protecting the stones from falling or reassembling them, whilst trying to bowl players out. The game ends when either the tower falls, or all the attackers are out.

One World Or None

Allison Whittenberg

Mama, how come you never told me about
the A-bomb?

Were we too busy
running from the men
with pillowcases and sheets
to duck and cover?

How come there's never
any of us in those
public service announcements?

They claim we can't get
a suntan, but are we also
immune to gamma rays?

Is it like flesh colored
crayons, something that
was created without
us in mind?

There weren't
whites only signs
on the air raid shelters
so I guess
they would
have
cracked
open
the door,
if we knocked
hard enough,
right?

We would have been
one
big,
at last,
happy family,
at the end of the world,
wouldn't we?

Three Epiphanies in Haiku

Wendy Miller

War Reporter

humans shooting at
other humans (exclusive)
stay tuned, more truth next.

New Message Received

Your texts don't send me
I'm on silent with you, over
due an upgrade.

Farewell my Love

long and prolific
I'm at the fag end now of
my smoking career.

'What a wonderful collection. Very smart and VERY funny. A stunning mix of measured wisdom and raw emotion. There's also a real sense that these stories – beautiful in their own right – belong together.'

Emma Jane Unsworth, author of *Animals*

TREATS
Lara Williams

Treats is a break-up album of tales covering relationships, the tyranny of choice, and self-navigation. This fresh, beguiling new voice paints a portrait of contemporary adulthood, balancing wry humour with a pervading sense of alienation in the digital era.

Williams' characters struggle with how to negotiate intimacy within relationships and isolation when single, the pitfalls and indignities of dating, dragged down by dissatisfaction. Meanwhile the dilemmas of life play out, including abortion, depression, extra-marital affairs, infatuation, new baby anxiety, bereavement, hair loss, sexual ethics, cats, and taxidermy.

FREIGHT BOOKS

freightbooks.co.uk

RRP £8.99
Released: 10th March
ISBN: 978-1-910449-70-7

Walmart Pants

Jim Ferguson

I'd just been for a haircut then I go into Asda for a new pair of troosers. What the Americans call Walmart Pants. Anyway it's really busy, folk mostly in for groceries. But the schools are due back after the summer break so there are a lot of women and weans in the 'Clothing at George' area, which is what they call the bit where they sell the clothes. They have men's, women's and wean's clothing, just about anything you could need though it isny great quality and the selection is a wee bit limited. You don't see a lot of men in here so I felt a bit self conscious. I thought I might as well get something simple, basic black troosers. No fancy design, bland as you can get really. I didny bother lifting a shopping basket which I think aroused suspicion among the staff. I felt like I was being watched. I flicked through the racks till I found a pair in what I thought was my size. I decided I'd better try the things on only to discover a massive queue of women and weans waiting to use the fitting rooms of which there were three. I felt a bit edgy in the queue mainly because it moved so slowly.

And no wonder it was taking ages, folk were going in with about 6 different items. I had other places to go and the main reason I'd gone to Asda in the first place was cause I didny think that it would be that busy. Also you don't get bothered with sales people trying to pap crap onto you that you don't want. Eventually I get into a fitting room, whip off my breeks, but I can barely get the Asda troosers up, I mean they're miles too wee. Miles too wee. So I get the breeks and shoes back on and out I go and find another pair, two sizes bigger this time. Of course when I get back there's a queue again, but a women with a wean in a pram, says 'just you nip in ahead of us.' 'Thanks a lot' I say, 'that's very good of ye.' This pair urny too bad, a wee bit long in the legs and a wee bit big at the waist but all said and done, they're wearable; black wae a Teflon coating. I fire my ain breeks back on, get the shoes on and take a look at the price tag. It says '£9'. I'm astonished at the cheapness. Of course they're no great quality but they'll dae me a turn. I convert the price into beer and it comes to 3 pints at pub prices or 12 cans of cooking lager from the off-sales. I'm a bit perplexed cause it seems to me that making a pair of troosers is far more complicated than brewing beer. According to the Germans beer only has 3 or 4 ingredients and by far the biggest component is water, which to the best of my knowledge isny aw that dear in this part of the world. On average a pair of trooser might last 6 months to a year, maybe more if you're careful. Three pints of beer might last an hour and a hauf. And they say time is money so where is the economic equivalence? Either beer is far too dear or the troosers are too cheap. At any rate this was enough to convince me that economics must be a very dodgy science. Then again you can get 12 cans of beer for £9, they might last a week at the outside, but for an average drinker maybe 2 nights worth. No hellish much beer really in comparison to what a pair of troosers does for ye. The trousers keep you warm, give coverage to vital areas and make you look smart or casual, for a reasonably prolonged period compared with the beer you can get for the same money.

No everybody shops at Asda of course. Almost no self-respecting teen would be dressed in any garment from The George collection. Because designer attire it is not... ...but then again somebody had to design the stuff, and humans are nearly aw, within certain limits, similarly shaped, so what's the job of these designers anyway if we're aw pretty much alike. Generally there is little call for troosers wae 4 legs or jackets wae 3 sleeves. And then it occurs to me that some poor soul on the wage of a dollar a day probably made these troosers, maybe in China or India, and working in conditions that would likely destroy their health in nae time flat. So it's a case of the very poor making trooser for the relatively poor and obviously Walmart and the transportation companies are making a profit out of this. I mean Asda or Walmart or whatever they want to call themselves aren't renowned for their generosity. Who ever actually owns them is making a bundle out of human misery. Plus ça change, as the French say. What can you do about it? Short of world revolution it's difficult to see any way out. Here we aw sit in tiny wee Scotland wae oor imperial British History and rest of it, no really giving a fuck about what happens to our ain men, women and weans let alone some poor soul in India making cheap troosers. I pay for the troosers and exit Asda into the Mall. I take a seat. A dude sits beside me and asks, 'Are you interested in meditation or the Eastern Religions?'

'Naw,' says I, in a rather abrupt Glaswegian manner hoping to discourage further questioning. But then the words, 'Liberation for the soul is it?' – come out my mouth like I wasn't in control of what I was saying. 'You're on the right lines,' says he. I screw up my eyes and look at his face because all of sudden my vision is getting kinda blurry round the edges. Like I'm in a sort of tunnel. I can hear this dude talking as well. He's saying a lot but I'm not really hearing anything. It's like my ears are full of cotton wool, and his voice has to compete with low gurgling, and high pitched whining noises in my ears. I begin to feel decidedly strange, like the whole world is receding away from me. 'Are you hypnotising me?' I ask him aggressively. But then I canny make out his reply, his voice sounds like boiling porridge, plip-plop-plip... 'Who says plip-plop-plip?' I ask and he gets up and leaves me there. My heart is beginning to beat faster and I canny tell whether or not I'm dreaming. I want to wake up and find myself in the hoose, in my own bed. Then I remember that I don't actually have a hoose and I live in a hostel for homeless men. And that I was buying a pair of £9 troosers on the off chance that I might go and try to find a job. I get this terrified feeling like I want to run out the Mall, but where to? But I canny seem to move, it's like my muscles are paralyzed and my senses are warped and weird. This is it, I start to think, I'm gonny die here, in a fucking shopping Mall.

The total ignominy of that for a death, and I begin to tremble so I tell myself to stand up. And I stand. But I don't stop shaking. Or trembling or whatever it is my muscles are doing. Though I know what my muscles are doing, they are exhibiting the symptoms of epilepsy. I begin to smell burning. I know if it continues beyond the burning smell I'll be unconscious and writhing on the floor with an overdose of electricity in the brain. I try to breathe. Breathe regularly, calmly, slow down the heart, try not to panic. Gotta be calm, gotta be calm, gotta be calm, I whisper to myself. I sit down again. I keep breathing. I try to keep the lid from flying off my cranium. Walmart pants, £9 a pair, Walmart pants, £9 a pair, I repeat this over and over like a mantra because I am interested in the religions of the East. And working for the wage of a dollar a day. Whatever way you look at it it's all good, all grist for the great human mess. The smell of burning becomes more intense and it feels like it's raining really heavy inside the Mall and it's foggy too. They have a climate machine to control the weather here, of course they do, then I see little specks of snow, only it isn't white snow it's black snow and I begin to think that this isn't epilepsy at all but the place really is on fire. The Mall is burning down with me in it. I can see sunlight and I run towards it. I come out the doors. I shout, 'HELP, FIRE!!' I hear someone ask, 'Where, where?' The air is fresh, everything is suddenly ordinary again. 'Sorry,' I say, 'there is no fire.' I put my head down and walk away quickly with my Asda troosers in their poly bag. I feel very tired, I need a sleep, and the homeless hostel is better than the street.

All But the Most Severe

Aidan Moffat

Common side effects, occurring in more than 1% of patients, include: itchiness, rashes, migraine, changes in taste, decreased libido or impotence, failure to orgasm, painful menstruation, tingling in fingers or toes, loss of memory or concentration, loss of memory or concentration, increased or lack of appetite, mood changes, anxiety, confusion, a fear of everything and everyone, yawning, indigestion, vomiting, stomach-ache, wind, immunity to booze (so you can't even drink yourself away), increased saliva, changes in weight, dizziness on standing up, a fast heartbeat, changes in blood pressure, runny nose, sinusitis, changes in passing urine, and dreams of death where the world's the wrong way round and you fall up into a bright blue abyss.

Uncommon side effects, occurring in less than 1% of patients, include: muscle pain, convulsions, increased libido, coughing, abnormal movement of the face or body, ringing in the ears, mood changes, slowing of the heartbeat, sensitivity of skin to light, sensitivity of soul to shit songs, allergic reactions, and fainting.

Occasionally, thoughts of smears on tracks or bathfuls of blood may occur or may increase in the first few weeks of treatment.

The Lady in Red

Aidan Moffat

Wait here, she said, and ran to the DJ. We were in the hotel bar, four boys from Falkirk and three girls from far enough away, at the last disco of the holiday, playing pool like pros and enduring the music. A few pints ago we'd laughed about songs we couldn't stand, and soon the distant drum machine and soft organ of 'The Lady In Red' tiptoes across the dancefloor, and the DJ dedicates the song to me: a special request from my holiday blonde. I don't want to dance but I've got no choice, she's got me by the hands and she's pulling me in, all swimmingpool eyes and sunblushed skin as we shrug along with mums and dads. The lights fade up and the bar shuts down, so we all take our dregs to the outdoor pool. And even as she lets my legs brush hers underwater, even as we dunk and splash and laugh, even as I replace the strap of her swimsuit *like a true gent*, I know that nothing's going to happen. Wrapped in stolen white towels, we walk back barefoot and pretend we'll keep in touch under only half a moon.

The Gospel According to John

Stuart Johnstone

Today's sermon is titled: get 'em laughing, and you've won a watch!

I don't know if there will be a test at some point but John's little homilies are accumulating and I can't possibly be expected to remember them all; I barely know what half of them mean, but I'm afraid to ask and risk looking stupid.

John is whistling, he's always whistling, or drumming, or both. Music seeps from him constantly and I doubt he even notices; I barely do any more. His cheeks are round and ruddy as if he is blowing with massive effort, but this is just his face, it will be the same when the music stops. On the night shift he takes his chanter down to the gymnasium while the rest of us play cards in the canteen. The distant whining notes peal through the empty night-time halls of the police station like the ghostly lament of a fallen Jacobite.

He showed me a picture once of when he was at the police training college, somewhere I've just come back from, my second and, mercifully, final stint, and he looked exactly the same. He would have been twenty but with his round jolly face and unfortunate hairline he looked like a wee old man even then. He won the Baton of Honour and in the picture he's proudly clutching it, the award presented to the outstanding new recruit in every intake. I hid my incredulity well, I hope. Part of the criteria now for this award is excellence in physical training, and John was almost as round in the photograph as he is now, perhaps the criteria was different then.

I am weeks from completing my probation period. Eighteen days to be precise; it waits in front of me, an invisible line like a nautical meridian which, when crossed, will impart status, respect and a sizeable pay increase.

John is driving, he has to. I won't get my driving course for another six months or so – can't come quick enough – John says often, I tend to agree, he fell asleep at the wheel a few weeks ago and since then I can't relax beside him. John was nervous I would say something to someone about it, he never said as much, but I know him well enough by now. Of course I *didn't*, I *wouldn't*. It's frankly unnatural to be driving at four o'clock in the morning. We should have been firemen instead, sleeping between cat rescues, lucky buggers.

It's a strange atmosphere today, but when does Christmas Eve ever feel like any other day, even when you're working. It has that last day of school feel, like we should be playing Kerplunk or Trivial Pursuit not heading to a call.

John is working tomorrow, I however got the day off; they needed drivers. It doesn't seem fair but John says he doesn't mind, I guess he's used to it.

We're pulling into the supermarket car park, it's raining but it had been snowing earlier in the day and the white lines of the parking spaces have been delineated with slush. John ignores them anyway and pulls up directly outside the front door. I know by now this means someone is almost certainly *getting the jail* as he would put it. He's made an assessment based on the information passed by control about this call.

We have an instant audience. I'm getting used to being stared at, something I struggled with initially and hadn't anticipated when I joined, but of course people are going to stare – it's the police, something exciting is bound to happen. I find though I am a perpetual public disappointment, things rarely get exciting; something else I didn't anticipate.

A member of staff has spotted us, one of the security chaps. He has a walky-talky and a look of embarrassment and relief. He shuffles to us and leans into John, so close I can't hear what's being said. I look around the place. It's crazy busy, we get called here fairly often, but I've never seen it like this, it's thick with bodies and fat trolleys. Some people are pretending not to look, pretending to linger for any other reason than to see the show, whilst others are just blatantly stopping and waiting for it to begin.

'He's locked himself into the security office, idiots left him alone in there,' says John out of earshot of the staff member.

'Who has?'

'The shoplifter. He's been smashing the place up for the past twenty minutes.'

Just as John says that I hear him, a small door secreted into the back wall of the supermarket and there's mayhem going on behind it. The staff are looking at us, waiting for the cavalry to charge, the shoppers stare on, anticipating. I'm looking at John. His hands are tucked into his body-armour, he's letting me get on with it. I don't have a clue, like most police work this one isn't in the manual, if there was one.

I put my face to the door and tell the occupant it's the police and to stand back. He replies with a hefty boot that leaves my ear ringing and my temper steaming.

'Fuck off, pigs.' comes his eloquent retort followed by the sound of a smashing bottle and the assertion that the first one through the door is getting carved open. Not only have they left him alone in the room but they also left him with the items he had intended to filch, including a six pack of bottled beer, now apparently converted to five plus weapon.

I spend the best part of twenty minutes trying to assert our position, but achieve little more than working the bottle wielding incarcerated thief into one hell of a lather.

The sweat collects on the back of my neck, this is not going well and the pantomime has gathered an ever increasing crowd of onlookers.

This has gone on long enough, I decide, and snap open my baton and reach for the handle intending to ram my shoulder into it and face whatever fizzing snarling beast comes at me from within. The crowd stir with anticipation seeing my preparation, and as I step toward the door John places a discreet hand on my shoulder.

'Here you,' he says drawing me behind him, 'If you don't stand back from that door, I'm putting the dog in.'

There's a brief pause, the banging ceases.

'*You've* no got a dug,' our shoplifter says eventually, but without conviction.

What happens next leaves me so embarrassed that I feel dizzy, physically nauseous like the legs could go out from under me.

John is barking.

It's an awful impersonation, but it's delivered with plenty of enthusiasm. There is a steady mix of incredulity and hilarity from the crowd. The laughter is boring a hole in my back.

'Down Killer,' John growls. 'Good boy. Last chance, neighbour,' he warns through the door.

The response comes oscillating with laughter.

'What the hell kinda dug do you call that?'

'Aye, well, he's only a Jack Russell,' says John, 'but he's trained to go straight for the baws.'

A full bellied laugh erupts from the staff, and from behind the door, I smile myself but I still yearn for the floor to open up and swallow me.

'Listen neighbour, what's your name?' asks John, his tone becoming more serious.

'Last name Off, first name Fuck.'

John approaches the door and lowers his voice creating as close to a private conversation as the circumstances will allow. I try to help by working my way between him and the staff who are just loving this.

'Well Mr Off, you know as well as I do that even if I wanted to I can't leave here without you, that's just the way it is and nothing anybody can do about it.

'You've obviously realised that you're going to be kept in over Christmas, and there's nothing can be done about that either and if I was in your shoes I'd probably flip too, but I hope I'd also have the sense to realise when I'm beat; 'cause although you're thinking it couldn't get much worse, we both know deep down it could, and we're just about at that point now.

'The only thing I can do for you is promise that we're only going to deal with the theft, whatever damage you've done in there we'll just... ignore. If you step away from the door we'll make this as easy as we can. You might not appreciate it now, but you will by the time you go in front of the Sheriff, I promise you that. Fair enough?'

Another pause.

'Aye, fair enough.'

I'm expecting a bear of a man to emerge from the office, but it's a skinny boy of nineteen who pulls the door open looking defeated.

Things are just as surreal in the car.

I sit in the back with the lad as John gives him a good talking to; his head hung low over his cuffed hands. He breaks into tears as he tells John he just needed to get his kids something for their Christmas, and John responds with a lecture on the proper way to provide for your family.

Then, lecture ended, John starts with the Christmas carols, drumming the steering wheel in accompaniment. To my continued bewilderment the young lad joins him in a chorus of Deck the Halls, the lad's voice still warbling with emotion through the fa-la-la-la-las.

'Get 'em laughing, and you've won a watch,' John preaches as he closes the cell door having handed the boy an extra blanket and a magazine.

Actually, now that I think about it, I do catch myself saying this particular idiom of John's now and again.

I still don't really know what it means.

Walking the Walk

Marek O Lasce

I cannot exactly remember when I first came across Tadek, but nowadays I consider him to be a close friend of lifelong standing. Both of us being involved in the theatre in many guises, we probably met during the staging of one of my early productions, in those far-off days when 'experimentation' and 'the right to fail' were integral to any forward-looking piece of drama. But this is not a story about me.

Even then Tadek was – and still is – a presence. Apart from his playfully mischievous blue eyes and an unruly mop of silver-grey hair, there is nothing remarkable about his appearance. He is of average height and somewhat overweight. He does not dress flamboyantly, nor slaves after fashion, yet openly admits that whenever he buys trousers he makes sure they are some three centimetres too large in the waist so that he can grow into them genteelly. Nonetheless, he exudes a magnetism that attracts people of all walks of life and of all ages, while he himself remains seemingly ageless. He frequents a variety of the city's clubs, pubs and cafés where he is forever made welcome and is invariably on first name terms with bar staff and management alike. It's not that he holds court in any of these known and lesser-known establishments, but if convivial, entertaining banter is to be enjoyed it will more often than not be found at his table, at which a place awaits one and all. Tadek can be either raconteur or silent observer as the mood takes him, and amongst his acquaintances he undoubtedly numbers professors, prostitutes, politicians, plumbers and pot-holers. Not to mention pimps and piss-artists.

There were times when Tadek and I saw each other on a daily basis, brought together either by work or for the pleasure of each other's company, but ours is a relationship (not wholly uncommon) that can bear years of silent separation simply to be picked up precisely where it was left off. So it was, that being involved in various international arts festivals, I happened to spend some months abroad. On my return, intending to surprise him, I tried to track Tadek down to one of his haunts, only to discover that nowhere had he been seen for at least a fortnight, if not more. This in itself gave me no immediate cause for concern. Gregarious as Tadek is, he is also very jealous of his privacy. A confirmed bachelor, though seldom at a loss for female companionship when needed, he lives by himself just south of the river in a well-ordered apartment whose threshold may be crossed by strict invitation only.

'I treasure my aloneness above all else,' Tadek has been heard to proclaim now and then. Undaunted, I decided to give him a ring at home – an ex-directory number handed out to but very few. I was greeted with a much disgruntled, 'Yeah, what d'you want?' But on hearing my voice his manner abruptly changed, 'Marek dear boy! How are you, no, more to the point, where are you?'

'Back in town,' I replied. 'Fancy a drink?'

'Sorry no can do, I'm not a well person, but why don't you pop round...'

'What's the problem?'

'We'll talk when you get here.'

'That bad?'

'No, but if you want to drink, bring your own. I'm on the wagon.' And with that he hung up, leaving me momentarily stunned. Illness and abstinence are not words one associates with Tadek.

The shock of seeing him when he opened his door to me must have shown on my face, but he merely gave me an enigmatic smile, and this in turn made him appear positively gruesome. He had, overnight as it were, aged a decade. His skin had an ashen pallor and beneath his eyes, which had lost all their usual lustre, there were dark, heavy bags. His cheeks were stubbled, sunken, and his jowls drooped merging with several double chins. He looked uncomfortably bloated and wore nothing other than a tattered, terrycloth bath robe, loosely belted and split all down one side. For a second we just stared at one another. Then he reached out to give me a hug.

'Marek you ol' bugger!' he exclaimed, 'so good to see you!' The greeting was heartfelt, though I sensed it was costing him some effort. At least he didn't smell.

'What the fuck's happened to you?' I demanded. Bluntly.

'I don't know,' he replied.

'What d'you mean you don't know?'

'Nobody knows... The quacks have poked and prodded and explored orifices I didn't know I even had. I've given blood samples by the armful, I've been photographed inside and out, connected to wires and machines, and I've been shoved into their dreadful scanners. That is not a pleasant experience, believe me.'

'And?'

'And zilch... they can find nothing. Nada! But I do have symptoms.'

'What symptoms?'

'Look, I see you've brought some booze. You know where everything is in the kitchen; glasses, corkscrew. I'm going to climb back into my pit... and I wouldn't mind a cup of tea if you can be arsed.'

'It's not the old joints is it?' I asked, but Tadek had turned his back on me and was shuffling off towards his bedroom. Either he hadn't heard me or had chosen to ignore my question.

I have long contended that Tadek's charismatic personality draws much on the off-handed way he infuses mystery into his background, his upbringing and many of his so called exploits and adventures. Apocryphal as some may be, not least of these are the accounts of a serious accident which befell him in Germany and about which he categorically refuses to make any comment. Though the details will vary in each telling, rumour and general consensus has it that it occurred at the dead of night in a private woodland and involved a Bavarian baroness, a Japanese gymnast, and a neo-Gothic folly in the shape of a swimming pool that had been drained of water. On one occasion, seeing him have considerable difficulties with his walking, he confessed that he had several crushed vertebrae and could count over thirty fractured bones in his body, some of which had not been set properly. As a result he has developed osteoarthritis in his knees and hips, hence my reference to his joints, but on entering his bedroom with a fresh pot of tea and an uncorked bottle of Chardonnay, I didn't think it relevant to press the matter.

Tadek was propped up on two pillows. The duvet was drawn up to his armpits and his hands were folded over an engorged stomach. His eyes were closed and were it not for his regular breathing he might well have been laid out for a wake. Books were scattered on either side of him, as were three ceramic ashtrays filled to overflowing. I am not a fastidious housekeeper, but it was obvious that for some time the room had not been dusted and the carpet neither swept nor vacuumed. Dirty clothes and underwear were piled on an armchair. A wastepaper basket spilled discarded Styrofoam containers and greaseproof wrappers from take-away meals. Fortunately a window had been left ajar and the air was fresh.

I poured wine for myself. Tadek opened his eyes as I sat at the foot of the bed. 'So tell me about the symptoms,' I said.

'Exhaustion, dear friend... He sighed. 'I have never felt so tired and so fucking weak in my life... whether I sleep or not. D'you know sometimes I think I'm not going to make it to the loo and back.' He sighed again. 'Then there's the vertigo... I can be walking, standing still, sitting or lying down, when without any warning my head goes into a spin. It's really, really scary, and can last from a few seconds to half an hour...'

'And the doctors don't know what it is?'

'Oh, they've thrown some acronyms at me, all syndromes of one sort or another, but nothing that can be officially recognised or treated with or without medication. I've virtually become immune to sleeping pills, and as for booze...' He dismissed alcohol with a limp wave. 'I'm beginning to think it's all in the mind. Though why I should be doing this to myself I haven't the foggiest. Even if it is psychosomatic, it doesn't mean to say that it doesn't hurt.' He reached for a cigarette and lit it, then clicked the lid of his beloved Zippo a few times. It is a mannerism unique to him and I doubt he is even aware of doing it. 'But enough of me!' he said, exhaling a plume of smoke. 'Tell me where you've been and what you've been up to.'

So I did. Much of my narrative seemed to be peppered by the kind of theatrical anecdote that seems to be the mainstay of many a television chat show. These cheered and amused him no end, involving as they did, a number of his acquaintances. At some point I handed him a mug of tea, while throughout we both smoked copiously. Then all at once I realised that my bottle of wine was empty and I was feeling decidedly light headed.

'Listen,' I said, 'when was the last time you went out?'

'I've no idea,' he replied, 'but I do know that amongst other stuff, Proust and that, I've re-read *War and Peace*... and it's still a damn fine novel.'

'So what d'you eat?'

'Junk food. The carry-out places round here with a home-delivery service are making a bloody fortune out of me. And then Mrs Maryla from across the way drops in now and again...'

'Right! Are you strong enough to get dressed?'

'Whatever for?'

'Because I'm calling a cab and taking you home with me. I've got a pile of videos you haven't seen and I'm not going to leave you here to vegetate...'

He considered this for a moment.

'All right,' he said, still a little uncertain, 'you're on. Go and see Mrs Maryla while I throw some clothes around and see if anything sticks.'

I did as I was bid and explained to his neighbour that I had invited Tadek to stay with me for the time being. She seemed greatly relieved and commented how much out of character it was for Tadek to be so absurdly depressed. When I got back he was ready. He had even packed a small hold-all.

After two marriages and twice as many children who have long since flown the coop, I have managed to retain the ownership of a large flat boasting several spare guest rooms. Moreover, my present partner (a pyrotechnics designer catering to all the city's major outdoor events) has a soft spot for Tadek, so there would be no problem of putting him up or keeping an eye on him. As proposed, for almost a week we sat and watched videos, anything and everything, from six to ten hours at a stretch – though I did manage to take time out to shop and cook. At first Tadek would emerge in the late mornings in that rag of a surrogate dressing gown, clutching it to himself as if it were some sort of security blanket, but he also had the grace to don pyjamas and a pair of slippers. Thus attired, he insisted, he was guaranteed a quick escape to bed whenever he felt overcome by weakness or a sudden onset of vertigo. Then he switched to wearing a track suit. Then he attacked my bookshelves. Within fifteen days, having read avidly, he started to dress normally. Whether it was the home cooking or not, colour appeared to be returning to his cheeks, though he was obviously still exhausted and somewhat unsteady on his feet.

'Time to go home,' he announced one afternoon, hold-all in hand. At a glance I knew it would be senseless to argue.

'If that's what you want...' I said.

'Marek my ol' friend, you've been brilliant, absolutely brilliant. Thank you. But now do be kind enough to call me a cab.'

'Sure. But you've got to promise me that you'll take care of yourself. Promise...'

'I promise,' he said. The smile was no longer grotesque.

I reached for the phone.

Soon it was our lot to go our individual ways again. I embarked on a lucrative summer schools' lecture tour of the United States and was gone for well over six months. When I came back I once more went in search of Tadek and found him in the first bar I entered. He was sitting with three very attractive young women, a tall tumbler of beer all but empty before him. To my relief he looked just like the Tadek of old, though perhaps his hair was a little thinner. He greeted me with a slap on the back and a bear-like hug. Then he introduced me to his friends, drama college students, but he did not resume his seat; instead, 'Ladies I'm afraid we're going to have to leave you,' he said. 'Marek and I have a lot of catching up to do, strictly boys stuff, one on one... so I bid you all a hearty goodnight.' And with that he steered me towards the door. Once outside, he said, 'Let's take a stroll down to the embankment.'

It was a night suggestive of a Golden Autumn to come, warm and balmy, and the not far distant river offered the prospect of a breeze. The pavement café tables and chairs were well full and for a while, arm in arm, we skirted them in silence. He was using a cane. Eventually, I said, 'You know it's really good to see you, you're looking so much better since the last—'

'Yes, thank you. I really do feel a lot fitter. And thank you for then also.'

'Nonsense, it was—'

'I tried acupuncture for a bit. It no doubt did some good, but I don't know... Perhaps I'm not patient enough... And then I met someone who whisked me off to the mountains. There I fell in with a bunch of very interesting people.'

'Oh yes?'

'Yes, they're into something called re-birthing-'

'You haven't found God have you!'

'Good Lord no! Nothing so trivial. No, no it's not a cult or a sect. No one's fleeced me of my ill-gotten gains. No, you see, they hire this place from the Highlanders, catering included, vegetarian and very tasty I might add.'

'You've lost a lot of weight.'

'That too. Regular meals, that's the trick.' He stroked the remains of his paunch. 'Anyway, these folk get into... self-help therapy I suppose you'd call it. Run by a psychologist. It's actually a lot of serious fun. And then there's the breathing exercises and of course the firewalking.'

'Firewalking?'

'Oh yes, bare footed across a carpet of burning faggots.'

'And you've done this?'

'Yes.'

'You must be mad!'

'That's exactly what I thought when I first saw them do it. They're a bunch of nutters... Six hundred degrees centigrade would you believe.'

'So what happened?'

'Nothing.'

'Didn't you get burned?'

'No. Not a blister, not a blush, not a twinge, not an itch, nothing.'

'But that's impossible...'

'It's all a matter of preparation. I've witnessed people getting badly, badly burned. You see, it's not a question of ignoring or conquering pain, it's all to do with overcoming fear.'

'But how?'

'A certain amount of ritual, a certain amount of frivolity, probably a certain amount of auto-hypnosis, adrenalin, breathing, I haven't got a bloody clue. But I will tell you this, it is amazingly euphoric... every time.'

'Every time? You've done this more than once?'

'Oh yes, lost count of how many times I've walked the walk... Listen, I'm not bragging. In fact thinking about it makes me feel very, very humble... Come on, let's get a beer and a nip or three.'

'No, I want to hear more.'

'All right... Whenever I feel that depression stealing up on me, whenever I feel self-pity tugging on my sleeve and starting to gnaw at my guts, whenever I get tired and weak and afraid of the head-spins, and whenever the arthritis seems unbearable... ' He shook his cane for emphasis. 'Then I say to myself... I say, Tadek... we can't be having this... after all, you can walk through fire...'

I turned to look at my friend. He was smiling contently into the distance, and I couldn't help but admire if not marvel at the spring in his step, the air of upright self-confidence that he exuded, and at the overall physical changes that had come over him. Yet what had really caused them left me somewhat perplexed if not downright dumbfounded. A healthy, ordered and regular diet was undoubtedly responsible for his recovery, but I was loathed to dismiss the fire walking. Perhaps in his case it had needed something that one-off, that bizarre and extreme to focus his mind, to make him realise that negligence, abuse and indifference had made an utter mess of his body. And as I began to seriously ponder the possibilities of my giving up smoking, Tadek's ebullient tone broke into my reveries.

'Well, here's our dear dear Vistula. The Styx of Eastern Europe. I haven't learned to walk across that yet, but who knows, I just might.' And he let out a guffaw that would have startled a bison. Then sauntering off towards the Towpath Bar, he gave my elbow a squeeze and said, 'Tonight the drinks are definitely on me... Żubrówka all round and no arguing.'

From *Beloved Poison*

ES Thomson

The lower operating theatre was as noisy as a cock pit. Wooden balconies, buffed to a dull shine by cuffs and elbows, circled the walls from sawdust to skylight. They were crowded with medical students, row upon row. These galleries were accessed by almost vertical staircases, up which still more of them climbed, and the walls were alive with chattering faces and flapping coat tails. Dr Magorian pointed Will to a chair overlooking the operating table. I sat down beside him. There was no better view in the house.

Two o'clock was Dr Magorian's favourite operating time – the light was not too bright and not too dull – though his audience had often been to the alehouse at lunchtime and the place was sometimes less than gentlemanly. Dr Graves and Dr Magorian stood in their shirt sleeves. Against the wall hung their operating coats. I heard Will take a sharp breath at the sight. 'My God!' he whispered. I saw his fingers tighten around the neck of the sack he held, and into which we had put the six small coffins. I took it from him and put it beneath my chair. I did not want him to crush them when he fainted.

'Dr Graves has performed ninety-nine operations in that coat,' I said. 'Today is the coat's centenary.'

'An auspicious day,' said Will, weakly.

Stiff with old gore, Dr Graves's coat had a thick, inflexible appearance, and a sinister ruddy-coloured patina like waxed mahogany. Dr Magorian's was worse, being as dark and lustreless as a black pudding. No one knew how many times he had worn it to amputate. It was said that he had stopped counting when he reached two hundred, but that had been some years ago now.

At that moment the door swung open and Dr Bain appeared carrying an enamelled bucket. He was dressed in white from head to foot.

'Avast there, Dr Bain!' cried Dr Graves. He tittered. 'Have you come to scrub the decks again?' The students laughed.

'What in heaven's name are you wearing, man?' said Dr Magorian.

'It's his nightshirt,' said Dr Graves. 'Are you playing Wee Willie Winkie?' The students laughed again, louder this time.

'What's going on?' whispered Will. He had perked up, now that something dramatic was afoot, and he was watching Dr Graves and Dr Bain with interest.

'Oh,' I said. 'Where Dr Bain is to be found, Dr Graves is never far behind – usually with a criticism or a caustic remark.'

'I met Dr Graves at the governors' meeting, when the demolition of the hospital was decided upon. He appeared... well,' Will hesitated. 'I don't wish to sound disrespectful—'

'Oh, you don't need to be diplomatic with me,' I said. 'At least, not where Dr Graves is concerned. He appeared resistant to change. Any kind of change. Is that what you wanted to say?'

'Yes,' said Will. 'Though his master, Dr Magorian, was equally vocal. Look at his face!' Dr Graves's smile was now a grimace, his teeth bared like an angry dog. 'Is he frightened, d'you think? Frightened of change? Or perhaps frightened of appearing foolish when confronted with circumstances he does not understand—'

'It's easy to ridicule what appears new and peculiar,' I said. 'Easier than learning how to think differently.'

'I agree,' whispered Will. 'And yet it's Dr Bain who intrigues me. He's standing before a crowd of medical students wearing what does indeed look like a nightshirt. Does he enjoy provoking his colleagues?'

'Sometimes,' I said. Indeed, now I thought about it, it was hard to think who Dr Bain had *not* provoked at some time or other. Not ten days earlier he had riled Dr Magorian by daring to disagree about the merits of pus in a wound. ('There is nothing laudable about pus, sir!')

'How fascinating,' said Will. 'And what d'you think is happening here?'

'I think Dr Bain is out to make Dr Graves appear a fool.'

'Oh?'

'Yes. Though I admit that at first glance, the odds would seem to be the other way around.'

Before us, Dr Bain was holding up his hands for silence. When he spoke, his voice was low, but clear. 'I have a suggestion, sir, if you will hear me.'

Dr Magorian, perhaps able to read the situation better than Dr Graves, waved a gracious hand. 'Proceed, Dr Bain.'

'I've been thinking about dirt.'

'Dirt?' Dr Graves gave a bark of derision, as if the subject were irrelevant. 'Ha!'

'Dirt, sir,' said Dr Bain. 'Put simply, dirt must be avoided. Especially when there's an open wound.'

'Well, I'd no more rub dirt into an open wound than you,' said Dr Graves. 'Nor would any doctor. Not even the young gentlemen of the audience would do *that!*' There was a murmur of laughter.

'Neither would I expect them to,' said Dr Bain. 'But there is dirt which we *can* see, and there is dirt which we *cannot* see. I advise that we must try to *see* dirt at all times, so that we know where it is. Only then can we avoid it. To wear these dark old coats is to hide it. To wear a white coat is to make it plain to see.'

'But you look like a baker,' cried Dr Graves. 'Or a half-dressed lunatic!'

'A baker wears white because he is dressed in old sacks. And it also happens to hide the fact that he is covered in flour. You wear a black frockcoat because you are a gentleman, and also to hide the fact that you are covered in—'

'Blood,' interrupted Dr Graves. 'Of course!'

'No!' cried Dr Bain. 'When it flows through the veins, *then* it is blood. When it has left the place where it is *meant* to be, *then* it is dirt. But we *must see the dirt!* For this reason I urge you to put away your operating coat, and wear one of these.'

'Excellent logic,' murmured Will.

'Rational, yes,' I replied. 'But I think it would take more than a white smock to show where the dirt lies.'

But Dr Bain was speaking again. 'I'm aware, Dr Graves, that you're about to undertake your one hundredth surgical procedure in that coat. But the greater the degree of cleanliness, the greater likelihood that suppuration of the wound can be avoided.' At this point Dr Bain produced from his bucket a brass spray-pump. I recognised it as the one I used in the small glasshouse at the physic garden. He turned to Dr Magorian. 'I have made up a 2 per cent solution of pine tar oil. If you will permit me, sir, I would like to mist the site of the operation during the procedure. Miasma, sir. Need I say more? The miasma too contains dirt, I am sure of it. It must be cleansed from the area!'

'Good.' I nodded, impressed by his thinking.

'What!' cried Dr Graves. 'Are we to be sprayed like aphids on a rose bush?' He looked about, expecting to be supported by the mirth of the students, but now they were silent. Dr Magorian, the great man, was about to speak.

'Miasma?' he said, raising a shaggy eyebrow. He sniffed deeply. 'I must agree that the river is at its worst today.'

'If we can prevent the miasma from entering the wound then the likelihood of suppuration is sure to be reduced still further,' said Dr Bain.

'We close the doors,' said Dr Graves witheringly. 'The miasma is kept out that way.'

'But we always close the doors,' said Dr Bain. 'And yet the place still stinks, and the patients still die.'

'Miasma,' repeated Dr Magorian. He stroked his chin, and waited for the silence to deepen. 'It is a curse upon us. I am willing to try your ideas, Dr Bain.'

A student leaped forward to help Dr Magorian out of his famous blood-blackened coat and into the white linen smock. Dr Bain held out the other. 'Dr Graves?'

Dr Graves snatched hold of the smock and dashed it to the ground. 'No!' he snapped. 'I am a surgeon, and a gentleman, and I will wear the coat that has served me well for so long.'

'But it has perhaps not served your patients well,' said Dr Bain. 'Will you not help us to see whether we can improve a man's chance of surviving the knife?' He lowered his voice. 'Come on, Richard! Experiment and inquiry is the life blood of our profession. What *seems* right may well be wrong. We must test alternative ways of doing things, no matter how absurd they may seem. Change is good. We cannot fear it or we must give up!'

Dr Graves looked up at the students. They had heard every word. Not one of them was smiling now. Nor could they bring themselves to look at Dr Graves. He turned around on his heel, peering up into the galleries, searching for someone, anyone, who might meet his gaze. 'What, no laughter now, gentlemen?' he shouted, 'No questions as to why or how this theory has been arrived at?'

The students looked down at their hands. Dr Graves took a step backward. But one of his boots had become tangled in the folds of the smock he had flung to the ground and all at once he lost his balance. He made a desperate bid to stay upright by grabbing hold of the table upon which rested Dr Magorian's surgical cutlery, and then, with a great clatter, down he went, to sprawl upon the sawdust amongst a confusion of knives, saws, hooks and clamps.

There was a moment of appalled silence, and then a great shout of laughter erupted from the audience. 'Silence!' bellowed Dr Magorian.

Dr Bain went to pull Dr Graves up off the ground, but the man staggered to his feet unaided. Sawdust covered his coat and trousers. His face was almost purple with rage, and in his hand he gripped a long curved boning knife.

Will clutched my arm. 'The knife!' he whispered.

'This is a hospital. Men hold knives all the time here.' I saw no reason for hysteria, despite the heated exchange taking place before us.

Dr Graves was panting hard; his hair was awry and his voice trembled with fury. He pointed the boning knife at Dr Bain. 'You!' he shouted. 'It's always you! You could just as well have presented your absurd ideas in private but no, you must have an audience. You are a maverick, sir, and you jeopardise the gravitas of our profession with your persistent nonconformity!'

'Dr Graves—'

'And when I do not choose to follow your lead in these clownish activities, you see fit to scoff at me beneath the gaze of my students. What professionalism, what courteousness is there in that? Dr Magorian,' he cried, 'you asked me to assist you, and I would be honoured to do so. But I will not do so if you continue to allow our noble profession to be ridiculed by *this man*.' His knuckles turned white as he jabbed the knife in the direction of Dr Bain. 'He will be asking you to wear your nightcap next!'

'An excellent idea, sir,' said Dr Bain.

Dr Graves made a choking sound. The students hooted. 'Gentlemen, will you *be quiet!*' shouted Dr Magorian. He motioned to me to pick up the utensils that lay scattered in the sawdust.

The uproar continued, but Dr Graves had now fallen silent. He was holding the knife tightly, his fingers wrapped around the top of the blade, so that his hand was cut and bleeding, though he appeared not to have noticed.

'Look, sir,' I murmured, hoping to help him save face, even a little. 'You've cut your hand. You can't possibly operate without first attending to this.'

I took the knife from him and pressed my handkerchief against the wound. Dr Graves gaped at me. His eyes were vacant, his face slack and defeated. He looked different, somehow. I stared at him. Something cold and hard, something dark, and filled with hatred seemed to be stirring at the back of his blank, glazed eyes. He blinked, and cocked his head as though he were listening, listening to a voice deep within himself that he had not understood before. Then he turned, and stumbled out of the operating theatre. The door crashed closed behind him. No one followed. No one spoke. I had been acquainted with Dr Graves for years, and yet, at that moment, I realised that I did not know him at all.

But the spectacle was set to continue, and the next moment the door opposite burst open and a pair of orderlies marched in. Between them they carried a stretcher, upon which was strapped a tall thin man of about fifty years old. He lay still as he was carried forth, but on apprehending his two white-clad surgeons and possibly thinking he had arrived early at the celestial gates, all at once he burst into violent activity.

'Calm down man,' roared Dr Magorian. 'Do you not recognise me?' He kicked the blood box around the operating table until it stood below the place where the patient's hip would be once he was in position. The patient was now wild eyed. He had been dosed with opium and alcohol, but he had caught sight of the table of knives and fear at what was about to happen seemed to have rendered useless all attempts to stupefy him.

There was a cry of 'hats off' so that those at the top-most standings could see. The patient gave a muffled gurgle. Dr Bain offered him a leather strap to grip between his jaws, and this he did, an involuntary moaning sound coming from behind his clenched teeth. The orderlies – burly men with hairless heads and giant hands – lashed the man's body to the operating table with thick, buckled straps. One of Dr Bain's dressers donned Graves's discarded nightshirt and took hold of the pine tar spray. Another eager student sprang down from the standings to man the pump in the bucket. Dr Magorian picked up a knife. A saw waited its turn. Beside me, Will was now as limp as a rag doll. He moaned faintly.

'Sniff this,' I said. I passed him a handkerchief. Hidden in it was a bottle of salts.

Will buried his face in the linen folds. 'Oh!' His head snapped back, his eyes streaming.

'Easy now,' I whispered.

'Oh!' cried Will again. 'Oh!' His voice echoed round the theatre.

'Mr Quartermain, if you could restrain yourself,' said Dr Magorian. He leaned forward.

'Mist!' cried Dr Bain. The students began working the pump and the aphid spray.

I saw the flash of the blade as the white flesh parted and a crimson flood poured onto the operating table. The students craned their necks to see. Dr Magorian's voice boomed out instructions, drowning out the dreadful muted screams of the patient, which soon evaporated into a whimper as the man lost consciousness with pain and fear.

Dr Magorian clamped the knife between his teeth like a pirate and plunged his fingers into the wound. The patient's blood stained his lips and cheek; his hands were coated in the stuff, his new white smock soaked from the waist. There was a glimpse of bone and gristle and red glistening tissue. There came the sound of the saw, and the *thunk* of Dr Bain's boot as he kicked the blood box forward, the better to catch the thick streams of scarlet that dripped over the lip of the operating table.

Will's face was as white as a corpse. Would he attempt an undignified exit, or simply crash sideways off his chair onto the floor? The first time I had witnessed an operation I had brought salts in my handkerchief and a pin in my pocket, just in case. I would not have had any of the medical men think I could not bear it. In the event I had not needed them – after all, was not blood and pain a woman's lot? Beside me, Will began to sway. I put my arm about his shoulders but he shook me off and staggered to his feet. He took one step in the general direction of the door, and then collapsed, dropping to the ground like a wet sack, recumbent in the bloody sawdust at Dr Magorian's feet.

'Get rid of him,' snarled the surgeon, his boning knife still clenched between his teeth.

I seized hold of Will's legs and dragged him aside. 'Mr Quartermain,' I hissed. 'Will!' I jammed my salts beneath his nostrils. And all the while came the rhythmic rasp of the saw and the faint *psst... psst... psst...* of Dr Bain's spray pump.

Then it was over. Dr Bain held the leg as it was finally severed, flinging it aside into the sawdust. Dr Magorian knotted the arteries, stitched the flaps of skin and removed the tourniquet. He stepped back from the table. 'Time, gentlemen?'

'Sixty-two seconds, sir,' cried a voice. There was a cheer. Dr Magorian acknowledged the enthusiasm of the crowd with a wave of his bloodied hand, though I could see he was disappointed. He had hoped for less than fifty-five seconds.

Beloved Poison, *published by Constable, is released in March 2016*

The Poetry of Science

Written for and performed at the opening of the Glasgow Science Festival 2015

Calum Rodger

Good evening – ladies, gentlemen – hello. I am a poet
An anachronistic job, I know – hell, everybody knows it
But please don't judge me with those relics from a bygone age
I love the work of Brian Cox, and my favourite Facebook page
Is – you guessed it – 'I fucking love science'. Truly, I'm besotted
As David Cameron is a lizard, as cream is best served clotted
For times have changed. The quill, the pen, have long since been outclassed
To quote the words of Coxy: *the universe is vast!*
And poetry's too... *human*. I think you get the gist
I've had it up to here with Shakespeare; I want to write like scientists
So ciao to ambiguity, goodbye poetic licence
I'm going to write a poem as verifiable as science!

So I went to see a physicist submerged in his equations
I asked him 'would you describe these as poetical, on occasion?'
He told me 'but of course! The purest beauty is in formulae
Second only to a triple-scoop with sprinkles chocolate sundae.'
I said 'that's my favourite too!' He replied 'well, great minds...'
I said 'whoa hold it, I'm a poet. I just came here to find
The most poetic thing in the observable universe
And given you're a physicist I thought I'd ask you first
Because physics is like physical, things and stuff, is it not?'
He smiled at me wryly and said 'step into this box.'
And there like a cat I remained and did not remain curled
For a month of chocolate sundaes in unobservable worlds.

Next I met a chemist who was working in her lab
I asked her 'what's the most poetic compound that you have?'
She answered 'this is H2O, the molecule of life!'
I said 'it looks like water', she said 'poet, you're right.
Two atoms of hydrogen are paired with one of oxygen
You'll find it nearly everywhere – it's very cosmopolitan
Without it we cannot survive – it's truly an elixir
But let me warn you now that it's rubbish as a mixer.'
'Permit me drink!' I cried, as she passed over the beaker
But there in my excitement I dropped it on my sneaker
So I grabbed a similar liquid, drank, and fell upon the floor
Dear God! It was not H2O but H2SO4!

Then I found a marine biologist, sailing on the ocean
I asked her 'what's the most poetic animal expression?'
Bottlenoses frolicked and plucked fish from out her pail
As she spoke to me of sonar and the cultural differences of whales
'What's most intriguing' (she went on) 'for we who live by speech acts
Is that they don't just get vocabulary – they even have a syntax.'
'But language is of men!' I yelled; she said 'that's rather sexist
And look – your casual misogyny has put the dolphins off their breakfast.'
I ate my words. She called out 'Ecco! This poet wants to swim!'
A spritely one leapt out the water and bottlenosed me in
I flailed around, regretful of my speciesist disparity
And could not have looked more foolish, crying 'oh the humanity!'

Finally I visited an expert in computers
Feeling in no small measure like an unsuccessful suitor
I asked him 'what's the most poetic thing machines can do?'
He answered 'everything you see! This world – look around you
Your phone, your journey home, the tablet that you're reading from
It's all computers. Everything is code! Zeroes and ones.'
'Incredible' I said, 'but surely one can't write
A poem made of only bits that wouldn't just sound trite?'
'Well try it' he said. I said 'yeah! I'll be like Neo!
One zero zero one one zero zero
Zero zero zero one one one one
One one zero one zero zero one!'
What fun! And though I'll still be using English in my journals
It has since gone down very well in avant-garde circles.

I got back from my journey, elated but tired
I had spoken in binary, nearly expired
Inhabited places whose existence is quantum
And got smashed in the face by a smart-arse dolphin
It was truly exhilarating, a cosmos of fun
If a little too vast for this ambiguous one
So I'll still read *New Scientist* and watch Coxy's shows
But I'll stick to the poems, and leave the science to the pros.

Rimbaud the Bampot

Andrew Rubens

(after Benjamin Fondane)

Here comes Rimbaud doon yer road
Brekin the grass in his haun.

Loafin. Like Whitman?
Like no man.

Not like you.
Leanin intae his unease.

Mad fir it tae be in contact wium.

Mad fir it.

Too mad fir you.

Ye cannae hudim.
Ye cannae pit words in his moof.

Rimbaud cannae hack it in the end.
Friendless. Freudless.
His confessions worth no more
than tavern songs, or witch-poultice.

Are you sure of yer real?
You infer wrang. Rimbaud
disnae want yer ways
and schemes for his
highways and dreams.

Rimbaud disnae want yer communion whites
Rimbaud disnae gie two shites.

Rimbaud's will is cast in iron.
Rimbaud's in fir it.

You hink ye ken hell but ye dinnae.

Scared tae follow his horrible work.

Scared tae follow his prints.

Scared tae end up burnin

a mute voice in the desert

limbless.

Tae a Sex-Toy

or, Scotland can gae fuck hitsel

Harry Giles

Wee sleekit, tirlin, purpie buttplug!
Come here n gie yer yampish slutbug
a keek at hou, like ony fuckdrug
      ye cheenge wir warlds.
Come in, faw til: wi doucest nut-tug,
        wir tale unfurls...

O buttplug, whan ye're in ma rectum
A'm plucked as true as string bi plectrum,
baith corp n pith as an electron's
      baith pynt n wave;
ye appen up a pleisur spectrum;
       ye mak us crave

a life whaur aw o thaim wi prostates
or ither glands whit want an onwait,
whas langsome sex-lives anely frustrate
      thair carnal needs
hae easins appened tae bullets, cock-mates
      n anal beads.

For trowe ye nou, for aw that sex is
but wan ploy in the offensive
for liberation o wir feckless
      fair fowk n planet,
hit's swank, hit's snell, hit's that infectious
      scads canna staund it.

Wad that wir heroes haed yer glamour!
Gin Rab the Bruce n Ed the Haimer
had kent hou ye'd reduce tae stammers
       the gabsie makar,
wad than wir nation yet be daumert?
       wir history knackered?

Sae pictur nou gin Willy Wallace,
a laird as macho as wis gallus,
teuk as his ettle no the phallus
       o swuird set swingin,
but insteid a puckered anus
       aw ripe fer rimmin.

Haed Wallace just haed ye, vibrator,
tae gie tae Langshanks steid o claymores,
wad than the baith o thaim haed catered
       tae the tither's lust?
wad rose n thristle hae masturbated
       til baith war dust?

Or think agin, did Bonnie Charlie,
feartie feck, the wan wha hairdly
kent the fowk whit he sent chairgin
       whiles he wis leggin,
get the airsewark lacked sae sairly?
       Did Flora peg him?

We ken the Brave kent well submission,
but no wi safewords or that fission
o bed fae body in positions
       o hole surrender;
dear buttplug, wad ye tak the mission
       o New Pretender?

A've lost ma drift... Ma theory's this:
that Scotland's happit in manly myths
whit grieve fer aw whit's lost, whit's misst
       bi defeatit glory,
but a Scotland sheuk wi anal bliss
       is anither story.

An, tho the yarn's mair fankelt yet,
whan homonationalism's set
tae neutralise wir queerer threats
       tae queen n country,
whan creative agencies beget
       a salmagundi

o pink poond chasin fads n fashions,
makkan aw wir slaurie passions
nocht but capital, but cash-ins
       on rebel grief,
whan roond ma sex-toys is that ashen
       haund o deith,

in spite o aw they monolithic
forces reenged tae quell the mythic
pouer o duntin up yer rovick
       a godemiche
A'm sure wi anal play wir civic
       dwaum's unleashed!

A ken that mair self-penetration
willnae really end aw nations,
or buttplugs spring th'emancipation
    o wir common weal,
but thay are pairt o the liberation
    fae deid ideals!

for tae ken yer anal passage
is tae win a better vantage
on the bonnie, quirkie marriage
    tween gie n tak,
tap n bottom, tent n ravage,
    free an brak.

Aye, whan A haud ye, buttplug purpie
as a thristle, A feel wirthy
o a nation doun n dirty
    wi buried treisur!
o a warld whit's free! n thirsty
    fer filthy pleisur!

Sae, Jacobites n Forty-Fivers,
drap the Saltire, wheesht the piper,
wash yer haunds, relax yer tichter
    orifices
n let yer buttplugs be the drivers
    o aw wir wisses.

Peace in our Time

Hugh McMillan

'I Left my Fish Cakes in the World's End'
would be a great title for a poem,
like 'Sheep are Hard Bastards',
or 'Thats what Happens to Porridge Sometimes.'
How much better than 'Adlestrop'
or 'She Walks in Beauty like the Night',
which make no sense at all in any world.
When I think of the titles of all the unwritten poems,
tripping innocently from tongues
under endless sun or stars, it makes me weep.
Look, we must, right now – Now! –
drop our spades and screens,
our cake forks and rifles,
and write the poems our titles need.

The Salon, Buccleuch Hotel

Hugh McMillan

Here are some artists.
They are thin and hands
move in their hair
as though the ability to talk
endlessly is dependent on it.
One is working on facial scars:
it is confrontational art, he says.
He has visited Glasgow
but the skin beneath the stubble
is unblemished and, framed in light
through tall windows,
he is like a Madonna,
not the sort that weeps blood.
They are happy to be forming
the narrative, their heads waggle
well into the twilight where outside
the day is dying.
I have sat here for many pints
waiting for the bases to be covered,
for the assurance I need
that the next step on the journey
will not be cursed, betrayed
or end in disaster,
and that if we keep them open wide enough
the sun will always pour from our mouths.

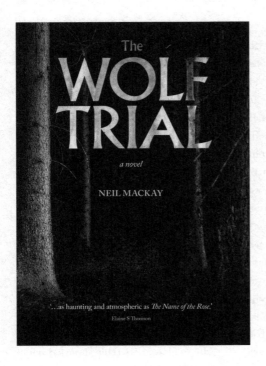

'...an audaciously imaginative novel, as haunting and atmospheric as *The Name of the Rose*, as beautifully written and finely plotted as *An Instance of the Fingerpost*... this is historical crime fiction at its very finest.'

ES Thomson, author of *Beloved Poison*.

THE WOLF TRIAL
Neil Mackay

If Hieronymus Bosch had written novels they'd be something like this. *The Wolf Trial* is a brilliant historical epic inspired by the true story of a man whose crimes were so great he was thought to be a werewolf.

FREIGHT BOOKS

freightbooks.co.uk

RRP **£13.99**
Released: 21st April
ISBN: 978-1-910449-72-1

The Rosebush Needs Pruning

Rached Khalifa

Who would have thought he would come home ten years later with victory and love? Not even his wife or children. Saddam Hussein is gone, and to her, in moments of intimacy, he would say in jest, 'You're my most precious booty in this war.' She would smile and reply, 'You're my Agamemnon.'

Her clever eyes smote his heart when he first saw her in Baghdad. The city was a heap of sand and sadness, more restless and dangerous than when under Saddam Hussein, but she stood out like an exception. Her sad eyes did not eclipse the beauty of her face. She stood in the street like a palm tree, slender and haughty, in a land wrecked by wars since time immemorial. The last one was waged by George W. Bush.

Her long black hair shimmered in the sun like the plumage of a blackbird. She was the only woman in the crowd unveiled. He liked that and interpreted it as a sign of her strong character. Her beautiful face stood out as a counterpoint to Baghdad ugliness in the wake of the war.

She spoke perfect English. She had spent many years in England, leading a life of student freedom and insouciance. She earned a PhD in comparative literature. She considered herself lucky, for her father was a general in the army, otherwise, her fate would have been sealed like that of any Arab woman who had no schooling–forced marriage, children, and a life of simmering death.

Two years after she was offered permanent lectureship in the most prestigious university in Baghdad, the Desert Storm came to blast off her academic dreams and premises. Saddam Hussein turned the campus into a bivouac for the Republican Guards, George Bush into a heap of concrete and mangled metal. In the meantime, her father died in the fierce Airport Battle, and her two brothers in Basra under British fire. This explained her wistfulness, he later deduced. He never told her he had led the Airport Campaign.

When he started dating her in secret, her mother was planning to leave Baghdad and live with her family in the Tikrit Province. It was safer there, she said in a last attempt to persuade her daughter. Nothing had been left that could keep them in Baghdad any longer. All was gone in the space of a few days–the sons, the husband, and security. Their luxury villa the regime had offered them, their fortress and pride, as she used to describe it, she would now sell along with the furniture, the garage, and the car. 'What will become of us if the Americans suddenly decide to withdraw?' she rhetorically asked her daughter. 'They will come and slaughter us like ewes, darling. Remember, we belong to the old regime. Their thirst for revenge is insatiable.' She said this with bitterness in her voice, for now she thought of Americans as saviours, not killers. That morning dozens of lives were chopped down in three simultaneous bomb attacks in souks and buses. 'Sooner or later, they will come to take their revenge, darling. They will never forget what the old regime had done to their families. They would have done it much earlier had it not been for the Americans.'

She dreaded her mother's plans and tried to make her change her mind, but her mother was intransigent. She had lost everything. Only her family and tribe could now give her solace, shelter, and perhaps also the desire to live on.

Her mother's face donned that sheen of sadness you see only in great masters.

What could she do in a hamlet beaten by mounting sandstorms and bigotry? What would she do there without her books and career? Since her return from England, she had seen her life degrade from civilization to barbarity. With the war, she hit the bottom. She had dreamt of international fame in comparative studies. She had dreamt of groundbreaking publications in renowned journals.

The thought of her life in the Tikrit hinterland sickened her and brought tears to her eyes. No way will she bury herself alive in that no man's land, she vowed herself.

He found his son waiting in the café, as agreed. Manhattan was bristling with contagious energy, as always. They landed in JFK at dawn. He took her to the hotel where he asked her to wait for him until he sorted out the matter. He told her he would see his son first.

'My children will understand,' he told her. 'I think they are emotionally prepared.'

'I am worried. I had a bad dream. Why don't you go tomorrow? Have some rest today. It's been a long haul.'

'My son is waiting. You should rest well. I will come back as soon as I am done. Wait for me here.'

She did not believe in premonitory dreams, but she had a rational explanation of them. What Freud calls an 'anxiety dream,' she argued, is in fact akin to premonition, for the self has its own way of transmuting inklings into oneiric truths. All happens unconsciously, of course. These hunches originate from the self's innermost mind which is in a constant process of scrutinising and analysing its surroundings. The synthesis of its analyses, she concluded, is what constitutes the dream-content—hence the intersections between dreaming things and living them in reality.

No one in the family understood what she meant, but they knew many of her dreams had come true. They dubbed her the prophetess.

Since he joined the American forces in the Gulf, things had drastically deteriorated between him and his wife. Through the years, their phone calls dwindled in number and duration. The rare conversations they had this year degraded to phatic communion and monosyllabic exchanges. He called her more out of duty than anything else. He had to ask about the children and if everything was okay. They've moved out, she replied. He didn't probe further. They are grown-ups now. They should lead a life of their own. His military upbringing taught him to value autonomy and discipline. Money was okay and the weather on Staten Island was okay too, she said. Excellent. Good. Yep. Eh. Okay. Okay. Nothing connected them anymore. They no longer shared what they used to share. She stopped talking about Daisy's funny feats. She didn't tell him Sasha had given birth to five lovely kittens and that it was time to spay her and that she had already booked an appointment with the vet in two weeks' time. What's the point, she thought? Oh, by the way, the rosebush needs pruning, she suddenly remembered to tell him. Get someone to do it, he curtly said. He claimed reception was bad in the desert. Same as here, she said. Bye. Bye. Blip.

'Is it your final decision, Dad?' asked his son.

His father looked much older than last time. His face was tired. The wrinkles around his eyes deepened and looked like tiny furrows in a muddy field. The desert took its toll on him.

'It is, my son. It's been going on for years now. It's time we put an end to the misery. It's better for all of us.'

He did not tell his son about his Arab fiancée. He thought it was untimely. He also did not want him to think she was behind the crisis. The matter was much more complex than what looked like a cliché.

He was particularly close to his son and his middle daughter. Unlike their sisters, he thought these two were mature and reliable. He thus felt more love for them. That they inherited the angular shape of his nose and the intense gaze of his eyes, unlike their siblings who rather looked like their mother, strengthened his love for them. He could see his genes in their features. When he was in the Gulf, they alone asked about him and sent him his favourite cookies. His other daughters never asked about him, as though he were not their father, which embittered him on top of his growing disgust with the war and with the sweltering heat of the desert. Sometimes he was almost convinced they had not come from his loins. They looked different and behaved unlike him or their siblings. What substantiated his doubts was their unflinching support of their mother in his disputes with her. Namely the eldest. His doubts seared his conscience in the darkest moments of his loneliness.

He was in and out the country on missions and in wars. He could not keep track of the insemination dates, as he put it to himself. When his doubt intensified for some reason, like a heated row out of nothing or a sudden prominence of an alien facial lineament, he would seriously think of conducting a DNA test to check their paternal lineage. Sometimes he envisaged sneaking into their room at night to cut locks of their hair and send them to a private laboratory. The results, whatever they might be, would at least bring peace to his mind, he thought.

Yet he dropped his scheme, for in moments of lucidity he thought it preposterous, if not disgraceful to himself and his daughters. What is the point? They have been raised as his daughters, and that is more than enough. Could genetics revoke his parenthood? He shrugged off the thoughts and carried on with his family life. He would ignore the row and turn a blind eye on unfamiliar traits.

Nonetheless, he still remembered how mean he was with his eldest daughter when she asked him for financial help to join university. He refused. She passed her exams cum laude, and enrolling at Yale was not a piece of cake. He was then getting ready for the Gulf. He said he could not afford it, though he knew he could. She begged him. She said it would be a loan she would reimburse as soon as she got a job. He was unmovable. He said he had other fish to fry.

He could not explain his callousness then, but deep down he felt it spring from some unfathomable desire for revenge or retribution or perhaps both. It troubled him to remember that incident. It was like an act of sacrifice. Shortly after, his daughter dropped studying altogether, married a wife-beater, and moved to no man's land in Colorado and stopped calling the family. His wife never forgave him for his callousness with her daughter.

He blamed himself, but mostly his wife. He should have been more alert since her sister, his brother's wife, ran away with that Arab. Her beauty was legendary. She reaped local and national beauty contests. Hussein came to prune the rosebushes. A few days later, they ran away together.

His brother was a rising magnate in North Carolina. He enjoyed great influence over business, politics and the media. When he came home, he found a laconic note on the fridge, 'It has to happen.'

He called the police. They later informed him she had taken a flight to Iraq that morning and Hussein was on board too. Airport CCTV footages showed them snug. She was wearing a veil.

His brother did not pay attention to the rumours at the beginning. He thought it predictable jealousy of her beauty and of his power. Since her elopement with the Arab, he espoused Republican politics and put his wealth and power at the service of the party. He supported Bush Senior in his Desert Shield and Bush Junior in his Desert Storm. He was frustrated when Bush Senior decided not to march upon Baghdad. For him it was a colossal mistake or at least this is what he said in public, but in his heart, he felt the victory fell short of what he wanted. Bush Junior quenched his thirst for revenge. He threw the most extravagant party in the country, reported the media.

When he complained to his wife about her sister's disgraceful frivolousness, she simply said, 'Have you not seen his paunch?c

Did she mean her sister had told her his brother was a bad fucker?

He did not know how to respond to her metalepsis. He swallowed hard and kept silent.

'What will you do then?' asked the son.

'Your mother knows I am back anytime. We will spill the beans this time.'

'I don't think she will be upset or even surprised.'

'It'd be better. I hope she goes for amicable divorce. However, if she refuses, I will go for it alone. She can keep the house. I am moving out.'

'She's changed a lot lately. She hardly calls.'

'I thought you are in touch. You are only a few yards away.'

'Not anymore,' his son said without venturing further. He had heard vague rumours but he did not want to upset his father or take part in smearing his mother's reputation. Anyway, they will fix it soon, he thought.

'If you need anything, Dad, I am here. You can always rely on me,' added his son, holding his father's gaze.

'I know, son,' his eyes started welling up, but he quickly rubbed the tears off with his palms.

He loved his father. He knew beneath his martial coldness lay a soft heart capable of compassion. Two years before, he brought a kitten from Iraq despite all the hassle of transportation. He called her Sasha. He said he had snatched her from under Baghdad tires. His mother interpreted it as an act of atonement for his crimes there. He is bribing his conscience, she ironized.

He contested his mother's interpretation. He reminded her how he had once saved a sparrow. He was five years old or so when his father found the baby bird in the garden. Its wing was broken, for it had crashed into the windowpane. It was a windy, slushy day. His father nested the fledgling between his interlaced fingers and told him to come along with him to find a vet. His father's hands trembled as he tried not to squash or stifle the little creature. The contrast between the bird's frailty and his father's thick fingers was oxymoronic, he recalled. The bird screeched and fluttered. He then handed him the fledgling and instructed him to lattice his hands like a small cage. They drove for miles in the blustery rain looking for a vet.

'And so what?' his mother shrugged her shoulders.

He lost hope in the civilizing mission in Iraq. He thought they came to bring democracy to the country, but as the days went by, he realized they only brought chaos and destruction. He was naïve. Al-Qaida was thriving more than ever in its new fiefdom. Death and violence lurked behind every corner, in markets, in schools and in mosques.

He whisked her off to a hotel in Kuwait, to a safe place where they could meet far from eyes and bombs. Her mother sold the house, the garage and the car and vanished among her kin in the desert.

They flew to New York for a new life together.

When he pushed the metal gate open, the hinges, strangely, did not squeal. They must have been oiled, he thought to himself. The garden was remarkably tidy, the rosebushes impeccably pruned, and on a perfect lawn lay the yellow clippers agape and alert like a scorpion ready to sting. Rosebuds shot out from shrubs like arrows, and the pale pink roses opened wide to the glorious morning sun. She had good taste, after all, he thought to himself again. His wife had insisted to grow only *rosa centifolia* in the garden.

He rang the doorbell twice. He could hear the chime echo back from the inside. No answer. He waited on the doorstep, hesitant and awkward, and then he inserted the key and turned twice. The door opened. An alien smell welcomed him, as though he stepped into a stranger's house. He walked in and closed the door behind him. There she stood on the landing, like a goddess on a pedestal. She had lost nothing of her beauty despite childbirth and menopause. She had even embellished during his absence, he noticed fleetingly. He always thought she and her sister had inherited good genes from their mother. She wore a black lace nightgown that fell short of her lovely white thighs.

She froze on the landing, her hand on the banister, and her eyes terrified and yet defiant as though caught in medias res of some act.

He, too, froze behind the door. He was thinking of something to say to dispel the heavy awkwardness of the moment when behind her appeared a man with a thick black moustache and curly hair, wearing his silk pyjamas. He was carrying a gun under his arm, his double barrelled shotgun, he noticed.

A crazy thought shot through his head. Maybe to defuse tension. He thought of kneeling and shouting like in olden drama, 'You have your Aegisthus. I, my Cassandra. Let us end the tragedy!' when a deafening detonation shattered his inner farce. As he felt his legs fail him, a vivid image of her waiting in the hotel room flashed in his mind, so vivid he thought a thousand neon lamps illumined his head. Then utter darkness.

Russel's Revolution

Lynnda Wardle

Russel hated Christians, especially Afrikaans ones. His theory was that we could right the wrongs of apartheid on the micro level. That was the way he talked: *Micro Level*. Russel and I agreed that the situation under the State of Emergency was making it impossible to live a normal life, but his strategy was not to hunker down and avoid contact as much as possible. His method was confrontation in the form of various *covert ops* as he called them, forays into the heart of Afrikanerdom and the apartheid state.

Lucas, Russel explained; it's no use making a big noise cos they'll fucken hear it. Softly; that's the way we infiltrate and gain ground. Then one morning these Dutchmen will wake up and *pffft*!! The whole thing will be bellyup. See, he waved an unlit joint at me, that's how true revolution works, bru. It's the Trojan horse principle. They sleep while we go in and do the damage. It's child's play.

Without intending for this to happen, I have somehow drifted into Russel's world, a world of semi-military confusion, grand schemes for dismantling apartheid and the paranoid mindset of a heavy ganja smoker. If I'm honest, sometimes when we're stoned, things seem a little less hopeless and his plans have a kind of humorous edge to them. I tell myself when we head off for another covert op that he may be right, it may not be the grand action that kills the beast.

So this is how we have come to this: we're crouched down early one Sunday evening behind a big hedge. The plan for damage this time is the minister's house next to the Dutch Reformed Church in the heart of Linden, a drowsy Joburg suburb with its well-fed middle classes comfy on couches, reading newspapers, sipping cold lagers and lazing their Sunday away. This is one in a series of attacks planned on what Russell refers to as *soft targets*. The dominie and his family, Russel explains to me, represent the bourgeoisie caught up in the ordinariness of everyday life, preaching the gospel of oppression, oblivious to the struggle of the oppressed. We are not the working poor, I point out to him, but Russel argues that it doesn't matter. Every revolution needs its intelligentsia bru, he tells me.

The hedge has enough gaps in it so that we can see the big windows facing onto the street, blank and trusting. No curtains, as though the inhabitants are confident that no-one might be crouched behind a hedge observing them; their lives, their property, planning a defacement of their Plascon white walls.

We tune in to suburban noises. Dogs barking, the stutter of an engine as a car pulls away in the distance. Enough noise to make this night seem just like any other. No blacks around at this time of night, except the servants, who will be safely confined in their rooms, no doubt plotting their own, much more effective revolution. When I point this out to him, he shakes his head at me like I'm some sort of halfwit.

You have to trust, Lucas, and know that every revolutionary action is a valuable part of the trajectory of the struggle. Trajectory. Jesus. It's the way that that the regime divides us, saying that you have to be black to fight the fight,' he says. We are all in this together china, and we have to see that. He slaps me on the shoulder. Come on boet, man up.

Sometimes I am silenced by Russel's philosophy, the sound of his voice rising and falling, flowing through my head like water. Knowing there is no point in arguing now, I stay quiet, scratching a spreading rash on my forearms, an allergic reaction to the hedge.

You got the spray paint? Russel gropes in his old army jacket for a torch. I give him the tin of red I bought from the local hardware store earlier in the day. Pay cash for it, he told me, so that there's no paper trail for the cops to follow. He has spent the day rolling joints and smoking, refining his choice slogans, writing them in pencil on the back of his cigarette packet. I thought *No Fight No Blame* pretty weak, but he liked the way it summed up a pacifist, yet revolutionary stance. What's yours? he asks, but I come up with a big fat blank. Dunno, I shrug. How about Working Class Hero?

We are on the move now. Russel uses the voice he developed when he was in the army.

Come! he barks. Follow me. No noise! This is it. Stage whisper, hand gesture, beckoning. We creep around the side of the hedge.

Sounds of a dog barking, suddenly very close.

Jesus! Russel hits me on the back with his fist, fucken moron nearly knocking the air right out of my lungs. Now he's bellycrawling using his elbows to drag himself along the ground. The ground is still wet from the afternoon rainstorm. I follow suit. I can see the ripple soles of his old army boots and suddenly I want to laugh. I have this feeling of shame and its making me feel nervous and stupid. We should just stand up, wipe ourselves down and walk away. We haven't done anything yet; we could slope off and no-one would be any the wiser. He looks like he's back in the Forces creeping through the veld on some covert anti-terror operation. I'm about to say, come on man, let's get the hell out of here, but he looks round, catches the look on my face and slices his finger across his throat, like, just shut the fuck up. The barking dog is frantic now. I'm thinking that it's likely one of those suburban kaffir killer dogs that will have no trouble in sniffing the fear off some whitey Che Guavaras creeping around under a dominie's hedge.

Russel!

Fucksakes man will you shut up!

I am a man in the wrong place at the wrong time. I know this with a clear and sudden certainty. I can forsee a terrible end to this mission: Russel and me running away from a snarling Doberman with bits of our trousers hanging from its jaws and the sound of cop cars hurtling around the corner. I am definitely not cut out for these types of covert operations, I tell myself. This is without doubt the last time I am joining him on his revolutionary recces.

The dog goes quiet. The silence is sudden and terrible. Russel waves his hand in the old army gesture of: forward men! We creep along the side of the house and still headsdown, make our way round the back. Now I can hear the voices from the church singing in wondrous chorus, the background music for Russel's revolution: Werk in my, Gees van God, skenk my 'n lewe nuut. Without irony, that is my prayer too: if I believed in God it would surely be for a new life, the gift of a life anew.

Russel has reckoned that there'll be no-one home while the dominie is pouring pearls before the racist swine in the church and he may well be right, but what if he isn't? What if his wife has decided to stay behind tonight and bake biscuits for after the service? Or the lighties. Maybe he's got lighties who went to the morning Sunday school and are now, even as we inch forward on our elbows, sitting in front of the television watching cartoons and sipping their cocoa? Russel's plans are so full of holes you can throw grenades through them. But he believes in the absolute cosmic rightness of what he is doing and, as such, has never come short. I, on the other hand, don't feel lucky and especially don't feel lucky tonight. This whole thing has got a very bad feeling and the feeling is somewhere in my gut.

Russel?

What is it?

I need a shit.

Ah, fucksakes man, just hold on.

Nah, I say firming my voice up, I'll just go and take a dump behind this bush. You go on ahead, I'll catch up.

He stares at me a moment weighing my integrity in the balance, and then he nods. Ja, the general has agreed to the plan thank god, and he turns away from me and heads round the back of the house. One last glance in my direction as if to check that I am not messing him around. I wave him on and give a thumbsup.

I stand in the dusk now, my insides tilting. Squatting behind the bush the tears come at the same time as the turd. I hang over my stink for a while bobbing on my haunches. The choir has started up again. That dog is still barking but now it sounds like it's further away. Maybe it isn't the dog for this house at all. Maybe the great man doesn't need a dog with all this hallelujah noise to keep evil away from the house of the righteous. I wipe myself off on a piece of crisp packet caught under the bush and stand up.

Flying ants swarm in the orange streetlight halos. I watch as they mass under the lights only to fall back onto the pavement, some dead, some squirming and wingless, some still able to fly and relaunch themselves again towards the light. I hear the tinkle of glass breaking. That must be Russel in the house now. I wipe my hands on the seat of my trousers and start walking down the garden path as though I belong here. Upright, not on my hands and knees. On the path in front of me is a half smoked stompie. I pick it up, light it. It tastes bitter and satisfying. I look around but no-one has seen me and I saunter down the street as though I am a man in control of my own fucken destiny.

Creative Writing

Carl Macdougall

Mrs Russell put her bag on the table then switched on the kettle before checking if there was enough water.

My cats, she said, as an apology and sat on the edge of the group.

Tom had been reading from his novel about a soldier with Robert the Bruce.

Seems a good point to interrupt, said Dave, looking up for my approval. I nodded.

Who gives a fuck about Robert the Bruce anyway? he said. Maybe I've grasped the wrong end of the thistle, but I don't think your average punter's too bothered about Robert the Bruce.

Then it's up to me to make them. And you have got it wrong. The book isn't about Robert the Bruce.

Aye, well, okay, maybe no Robert the Bruce, but the point I'm making is that historical fiction is, by its very definition, unreal.

His comments were addressed to Karen, who was staring at the floor.

Have you finished swearing? asked Mrs. Russell.

Don't tell me you're going to start.

It was a question. And I very much doubt if anyone could tell you anything.

Was that the end of a chapter? I asked.

I'm not doing chapters, just sections. I think it's more impressionistic.

Can I have some comments?

It's very good, said Betty, who nodded while Tom was reading.

Aye, well, it's good right enough, for what it is, but it seems to me the question is not what it is, but what it could be. What do you think, Karen? asked Dave.

I think it's interesting. I don't know much about history, but hearing something like that makes it come alive.

Anyone else? I asked. Or can we move on?

Could you do mine? said Mr. Anderson.

Mrs Russell sighed. The kettle's boiled, she said.

Other people have to read, said Mr. Anderson. I'll do my piece.

Telephone banking is a fad and further evidence of the way standards are slipping in today's banking world. To my mind, nothing can replace the cheery teller who knew you and who was part of the same community as yourself. Cash machines and telephone banks may be part of today's society, but, just as junk food is replacing 'halesome fairin' and if scientists are to be believed we are paying the cost in obesity and anti-social behaviour and folk are having to be taught to make soup and eat salad, then society will surely come to rue the day it closed the local bank and replaced the ledger with the computer.

Were you made redundant when your branch closed? asked Dave.

I was happy to take early retirement.

Mrs. Russell was staring at the floor. She looked away when Mr. Anderson asked for comments.

It's very good, said Betty. Makes you think.

And what about you? he asked. Would you like to comment?

I stopped listening, said Mrs. Russell. It was very boring.

Are you German? he asked.

You've asked before and I've told you. I'm from Yugoslavia, which no longer exists.

I thought you were German because you cannot pronounce the letter *r*. My wife and I have had many happy holidays in Austria. The Tyrol is lovely. Still, if you are not from here you won't be familiar with the issues raised in the letter, will you? And what about you Tom?

Fine, sure, yeah, great.

What does that mean? Did you like it?

Yes. It was very good.

And what about the teacher?

It seems to me that with a little time and thought it could easily be developed into a short article. There's a touch of reminiscence, which could be expanded; you know the sort of thing, local branch, high counters, open fires, all of that. But I don't think it's publishable as it stands.

You said that before and the letter was published. In fact, the editor thought it was very good and asked for another letter.

Well, I could be wrong again.

I mean, it's only your opinion.

Which is what you asked for and if that's not what you want you'll have to ask yourself why you're here.

Betty read three verses of a poem on how she felt when she looked at her granddaughter, wondering if the child would remember her.

What do you think, Dave?

Yeah, well, it's very interesting.

What's interesting about it?

The fact that she's tried to articulate what she feels.

And why should that be interesting?

Maybe Tom could tell us if he likes it?

I wouldn't like to interrupt your train of thought.

I asked my husband what he thought and he said he liked it very much, said Betty. Dave's right. I tried to express what I felt and I'm glad that comes across?

Yes, said Dave, Of course it does. How does that sound to you, Karen?

I liked it. I understood it. I'm not a grandmother, but I am a mother and I can understand she would feel these things about a baby.

She isn't a baby. She's nearly three.

But surely everyone feels these things.

Of course, said Mrs. Russell. What you are avoiding is that this isn't a poem at all. It has no form and very little content. It is sentimental and embarrassing. Why come here if you only want to hear everything's fine. Don't you want to improve? Surely you don't want to keep on producing the same standard all the time. Surely you want others to think you are capable of doing more.

We never hear you read anything, do we?

I must agree, said Mr. Anderson. I find your comments distinctly unhelpful, given the fact that you don't contribute anything yourself.

I believe in telling the truth, she said. But you wouldn't understand that.

Two weeks later the librarian gave me an envelope.

Isn't she coming back then? Tom asked.

I'm not sure. I'll read this and get in touch.

I have a new poem, said Betty. And I've started a story. Perhaps you'd like to read it. It's just a page.

We'll do it when it's finished.

I'd like to read an article I've done for the local paper, said Mr. Anderson. It's about fishing. It's called 'The One That Got Away' and I've handed it in.

I'm thinking of writing a novel, Mrs. Clark told Tom. This was her second class. She'd told Dave to wash his mouth out. He told her to fuck off and hadn't been back. Karen phoned to say she wouldn't be at the class: baby sitters.

Has anyone else brought work? I asked.

I've had a letter from a publisher saying they've accepted the manuscript, said Mrs. Clark.

Do you mean received?

It's very expensive, sending it round like that. Is there no other way? Perhaps you could send it to your publisher. I'd let you read it.

I think we should start, said Betty. I'll do my poem. It's called 'A Rose.'

Mrs. Russell used a manual typewriter and single spacing. The page numbers were written in blue ballpoint on the top right corner. She had added sentences down the side of the page with postscripts and additions on the back of receipts and handouts. There was often little or no connection between the paragraphs.

What difference does it make? I married him. He was happy. I got his name and a passport and he got me.

I wanted to be someone other than who I was. And now I am Mrs Russell, though I am also what I have been. How can I tell who I was and what I became? I would have to lessen the Story, would have to make it happen to someone else to make it believable, yet it happened to me.

And I knew; from the time they came into the courtyard, I knew. The tall one who never Spoke, looked at me and grabbed my dog, Mitzi, a small dog, silly and always barking when she wanted to play. I said, 'Quiet, Mitzi.' But she kept barking.

He bent down and Stroked her and when she Started jumping as if to play he held her by the skin at the back of her neck, held her in the air like a sack, took out his gun and shot her head off. Then he looked at me and I knew. He was holding the body of the dead dog and his arm, his clothes and the side of his face were covered in blood. The others laughed. But he did not laugh. He looked at me and I knew, knew not to cry or to let him see it affected me in any way.

Even when they held me down in the yard, two men kneeling on my arms, two holding my legs and one on top, changing places, taking turns, even then I didn't cry.

They were machines, animals in the arts of pillage and brutality, loving nothing but Strength and believing in nothing but their own superiority and their right to do whatever they liked to those they considered inferior to themselves, which was everyone.

Now others ask, Why? Why didn't you do something? What could we have done? We were viĉtims too. Which avoids the shame of having done nothing, denigrates the achievements of those who tried, however trivial, and denies the faĉt that they put themselves in that position, courted and accepted it willingly. No one did it to them. They did it to themselves and cannot accept the shame.

Karen said, I need to see you.

She was dark-eyed and tall with narrow shoulders and long legs. I liked the way she always looked neat and Straight, almoSt regal. She never wore make up and her skin had a slightly tanned appearance.

It is not unknown for people in my position to have affairs with folk who come to the class and I wondered about me and Karen, walking through a silvery rain in the Spring sunshine. She was waiting when I arrived. She looked untidy, drawn and tense and Started talking immediately.

I have to tell you what's happened, not because I'm frightened or ashamed, but because I have to tell someone and you're the only person I truSt who knows us both. Did you know I'd broken up with Benji's dad. I told Dave what happened, one night after the class we went for a drink. I saw him a bit later and he's written it up as a Story.

Robert the Bruce's soldier had fallen for a beggar girl and was dreaming of a future, though he was disappointed when he saw the Bruce, who was small, bald and fat.

I don't know what to do with him, said Tom. I feel there should be more to him, something that seems more typical of his time. I don't feel he's real enough. Something needs to happen to make him more realistic.

Mrs Clark's novel had been rejected, but she'd heard from a magazine: If I rewrite the story they'll publish it, she said.

And a poem had been accepted for an anthology she'd seen advertised in a women's magazine. Copies of the book cost £35.00. Does anyone want to buy it? she asked.

Mr Anderson had written *How Lucky We Are To Have Local Libraries*.

However, he said, I have something far more interesting.

I've seen this, said Tom. I know what it is and I don't think it has any place here. It has nothing to do with this class.

I beg to differ. I think it has everything to do with the class. So much so that I have taken liberty of photocopying it.

Tom gathered his stuff.

This concerns someone who used to come to the class, he said, and is no more than a series of allegations. You've no right bringing it here and it's difficult to think you've done this out of anything other than malice.

A Sunday newspaper reported that the Bosnian authorities had applied to the British government for Mrs. Russell to be extradited to face charges brought by a new state prosecutor. A commentator said there was a strong political element: the government was in economic difficulties and this could divert attention and go some way in restoring a sense of national unity. At best, it was a diversionary tactic.

The story alleged that as Dijana Dizdarevic in 1993, in the municipality of Konjic in Bosnia and Herzegovina, Mrs Russell had taken part in the massacre of 22 Croat civilians and eight prisoners of war. She and five other members of the Zulfikar special unit of the Bosnian army carried out the attack. The victims were killed by firing squad and she had been identified from photographs.

The article said Mrs Russell was a Muslim, that she lost several members of her family in the conflict and was the victim of a wartime rape. She was willing to testify against the other participants, to provide the court with all information and evidence relating to the attack and had expressed remorse to the relatives of the victims.

The matter was in the hands of the Foreign Office where no one was available for comment, though it was expected she would be extradited.

I arrived after midnight. I thought of putting a packet of cigarettes through the letterbox and leaving a bottle of wine on the doorstep, but if reporters had been hanging around, it could have given the wrong impression.

The house was dark. When I knocked, I thought I heard a movement behind the door.

It's me, I said. Mrs. Russell, it's me.

She lived in a basement that seemed darker than the street. It took time to adjust to the low ceiling and dim light bulb struggling against the confusion and the smell.

Excuse the mess, she said. My cats.

There was a small sitting room with a sofa and a blanket of coloured crocheted squares over the back.

She brought through a tea plate with salad and a hard boiled egg in slices. We ate facing each other with the plates on our knees, drinking from a bottle of pale red wine.

The lamp and gas fire were the only lights in the room. I was aware of a bookcase at my back and a dresser to the left. Her chair was beside the fire, facing the television.

She had known for some time, sent everything she had to the judge who was handling the case and had still to hear about her extradition. The paper told her they were running the story and asked for a comment.

At first, the phone barely stopped ringing, but the people outside had gone away. Now there are calls during the night, at three and four in the morning. No one from the Foreign Office had been in touch.

I take it the story's true?

What difference does it make? We did what we had to do to survive. Everyone is guilty. If this story is true, am I more or less guilty than the woman who gave her daughter to the soldiers, who sold her body for nylon stockings or chocolate bars, the men who dug the pits or the boy who drove a wagon, knowing what was in it, the thousands who say they never saw or heard, the people who looked the other way?

She drank as she talked. Twice she finished a bottle and came back with another, pouring a drink when her glass was empty, tilting the bottle in my direction. She drank at least twice as much as me and seemed to smoke continually. Her voice was low and flat, deliberate, as though she was reciting something she had been forced to learn.

It sounds silly, she said. It's no defence, not really. But I cannot remember what I was like when I was a teenager. Who can? Do we not do things then of which we are later ashamed, especially women? Do we let them overtake us? Do we sit and mope and continually make amends, or do we try to put the past behind us and get on with it. What about you, have you led a blameless life?

I've never murdered anybody.

Then you are very fortunate. Do you, does anyone think I walked away unharmed? I ignored the pleas of the men who got down on their knees in front of me, I heard the children's screams and have tried to obliterate them, but nothing works.

You're not seriously suggesting you had no choice, that you're a victim?

No. I made choices that were based on my opinions and experience, on my greed and ambition, like everyone else. I knew what I was doing and I believed in the things I did, otherwise I couldn't have done them. And seeing it now, looking back, I don't blame anyone else; I'm not saying I was innocent. I am saying I was wrong. Part of me hopes they kill me. But they won't. They'll send me to prison and rehabilitate me. I don't care and I've never cared. They say I've been dehumanised and perhaps they are right.

By now she was drunk. She slept, suddenly waking and staring at me, then lapsing back to sleep. I sat for a while, listening as she muttered and dreamed in a language I did not recognise.

I put the crocheted blanket round her, turned off the fire and the light and walked home, thinking of the small clump of daffodils and bluebells that bloomed every spring by the side of the A85 to Oban. I first saw them as a child and looked for them every time I passed. The house had gone, but the daffodils remained, blooming every year.

Dave brought a story.

I wondered if you'd take a look, he said.

Run up a few copies and we'll do it in class.

You might want to look at it first.

No need. We'll do it in class.

Mr. Anderson was about to read his article on recycling when Karen arrived. Her skin was shining, slightly darker than usual and she'd put a little make up round her eyes. The light caught her hair. She had a short dress below her raincoat and raised heels. She sat opposite Dave, smiled at me and crossed her legs.

It occurred to me that we used to throw out our rubbish, Mr Anderson said. "Now we have to keep it.

It's very good, said Betty.

Yes. It seemed an unusual subject. Something I could get my teeth into. I like something like that, slightly unusual. Have you brought your story?

No, said Betty. I'm still working on it.

It would be good if you could do something slightly different.

I'm going to put a twist in the tail.

Very good. I'll look forward to hearing you read it?

Tom's soldier had been wounded at Bannockburn and taken to Inchcolm Priory. When his injuries healed he went to Stirling to find the girl, but no one had seen her. It took him five days to reach Edinburgh where he met her brother, who was working for an apothecary who had seen her with a soldier from Edward's camp heading across Minch Moor. She was probably in England.

It's very sad, said Betty.

I reckon people were pretty much the same then as we are now, said Tom. They did what we do and felt the same things.

Perhaps not so sophisticated, said Mr Anderson.

I don't think we're sophisticated, said Tom.

Mrs. Clark had entered a competition called Memories. She brought in a couple of poems and a story about the Fair Friday her father came home drunk, having lost his pay. The poems were about the people who lived beside her and the way the city had changed, how, walking down Buchanan Street she remembered what used to be there.

I suppose we've all heard about Mrs Russell? Dave said to no one at the interval.

The matter's been fully investigated here, said Tom.

I followed the story fairly closely, Mr Anderson said, and it just faded. There was the Sunday thing, then the dailies picked it up, but it was dead by Wednesday. By the way, I don't know if anyone picked up on the fact that she was a Muslim.

Just shows you, said Dave. You never know.

Never know what?

You never know who you're dealing with.

She was always an outsider, said Mr Anderson, never really one of us. There were no subtleties about her. She was too direct, too anxious to hurt someone's feelings.

What happens if she comes back?

She won't come back. She can't.

Why not?

Well, for one thing I expect she'll be sent back to where she came from and will spend some time in jail. Apart from that, she wouldn't be welcome.

Is that because she murdered people or because she didn't like your work?

Her opinions meant nothing to me. I simply don't want to associate with someone like that. But it isn't up to us to say whether she should be here or not. Surely it's up to the teacher.

I rather liked her, I said. I thought she livened things up a bit.

I'm not sure I understand what you mean, said Mr Anderson. Did you agree with what she said?

Not always, no; but some of the time, of course.

I agree, said Tom. I think Mr Anderson would like to shut her up because he didn't like what she said. Is it her past you object to?

It's a matter of conscience. We have to make a stand. She has to know we do not approve of what she did.

What makes you suppose she might think otherwise?

I'm sure she doesn't. But I don't think we should be seen as sympathisers.

Just because she comes to a writing class doesn't mean we sympathise with her views or approve of her past. She may have changed for all we know.

That would be convenient.

So whether she has changed or not, you still won't believe her. Isn't that a policy she might have supported?

You misunderstand me. I was thinking of writing about it," said Mr Anderson, putting my views on paper as a record. I think someone has to be clear.

What about you, Dave? I asked. Will you be putting your views on paper?

No.

Have you copied your story?

Are you going to read a story? asked Karen.

No, he said. It isn't finished. Not really. It's just a few notes.

What a shame, said Tom. We've waited so long. What's the story about?

It isn't finished.

Perhaps the atmosphere might be a bit hostile, said Karen, especially if you don't know what you're dealing with. If there's nothing else, no other work, I've got a story.

I'd like to hear it, said Mr Anderson.

Her voice was strong and confident. She faced Dave, glancing up every now and then, as though reading to him.

I invited Lily to stay for a few days. Brian phoned to ask if he could visit.

My boyfriend went off to see his friend who had a pub outside Arbroath. Or maybe it was when he had the pub in Aberdeen, the one that was supposedly haunted by the ghost of a workman who had died installing the service lift, who slammed doors and walked along the upstairs corridor.

I bought bottles of wine. They brought bottles of wine. Lily brought me flowers with a little card tucked inside: To my best friend xxx.

We drank the wine. Every so often, Lily and Brian would look directly at each other. When Lily went through to the kitchen to have a cigarette, Brian and I kissed. Lily came back through and started crying. I put my arms around her. She disappeared again and came back wearing a black silk camisole over her jeans. She was flat chested, almost like a boy.

She'd slipped a strap down below her shoulder. I went to change into my pink silk teddy. The evening seems like a series of events without a soundtrack. We went through to my bedroom. As the three of us slipped under the duvet, I thought of the mess of bottles and cigarette butts back in the living room. Brian lay on the left of the bed, Lily in the middle, me on the right. Lily and I kissed. I could feel her legs brushing against mine. They were bristly and I didn't want to touch them. Brian was irritated.

Are you just going to ignore me? he said.

Lily and I fumbled for a bit. Then a wave of utter loneliness swept over me. I turned over, my voice muffled by the pillow.

Go to the spare room. I want to sleep.

They left. I grabbed my large stuffed rabbit with the pink ribbon and cuddled into it. I think I cried for a bit, then fell asleep.

The next morning I got up about 10, hungover and puffy eyed. The door of the spare room was closed. I made a lot of noise, slamming the door on my way out to get a Sunday paper, then clattering crockery when I got back and made myself a cup of tea.

The spare room stayed closed. I grabbed my keys and caught a bus into town, leaving the previous night's wreckage to be dealt with later.

When she finished, Tom was smiling. There was a stillness rather than silence, as though they were waiting for something that would allow them to continue.

Names have been changed to protect the guilty, Karen said. Or rather, one of the names has been changed. I don't know why. Couldn't really bring myself to write the guy's name.

Does anyone want to say anything?

I loved it, said Tom. And I wanted more. I don't really have anything else to say.

I'm not sure I found the subject suitable, said Mrs Clark.

I know what you mean, said Betty.

I mean, it was well enough written and all that, very compelling, but not what I want to hear. There's enough of that sort of thing on television, isn't there.

What does Mr Anderson think? asked Tom.

Well, it's another world, isn't it?

Not really. You have no views on loneliness and despair?

I don't think that's the sort of thing I want to hear. There's enough of it in the newspapers and, as Mrs Clark says, it's also on television. What does the teacher think?

I'd like to hear Dave's thoughts.

Yeah. It's good. It's the best thing she's written.

Do you want to do your story?

No, I'll leave it.

Tom and I went for a drink.

Wee celebration, he said. Finished the book, sent it off and now we wait and see what happens.

While working on another?

He smiled.

So you won't be back?

I don't think so. It got me started and made me think about what I wanted to do. By the time I got home I'd decided to leave.

What are we going to do? said Betty.

We'll have to find someone else, said Mrs Clark.

I have a short piece, Mr Anderson said. Nothing important, of local interest only, perhaps you could do it before you go, since this is your last class. It's on immigration.

I don't think I've anything to say, I told him five minutes later, other than to tell you with some relief that I disagree with every sentiment it both expresses and suggests and it's what it suggests that's most disturbing.

I was wondering, he said. If we don't get a replacement tutor, could we send some of our stuff on to you, just for your own interest and perhaps you could write a comment or two on each piece.

That's a good idea, Mrs Clark said.

No. That won't be possible.

That night I read the opening half dozen pages, finishing with how Dijana Dizdarevic became Anna Russell, the website, her husband's visit to Sarajevo, her marriage, his family's disapproval and, finally, divorce.

I'd always longed for a permanence I could believe in; even when I was miserable, I was afraid of losing what happiness I had. This week, next week some time soon, it would happen, the skies would open, the blight would come and I'd be struck. The only certainty was death, far more certain than God; and though I envied those who believed in God, I could neither accept nor understand their trust, far less throw my hopes upon uncertainty.

Next day I phoned. I tried at least three times in the following days and was eventually answered.

My name is Jackie, the voice said. I'm with the social work department. The previous tenant has given up the flat and we're clearing it for reletting.

I asked if there were papers.

Papers?

Like a manuscript?

We cleared everything out. We got rid of a lot of papers, and, to be honest, none of the furniture or bedding was worth keeping, so we dumped the lot.

Just before Christmas I met Karen in a department store.

Isn't this awful, she said. Christmas shopping. Why do we do it?

How are you?

Good. What about you? Do you still take that class?

No.

Is it still going on?

I've no idea. Are you thinking of going back? Have you been writing?

Not really. I only did that stuff for the class. I think I was going through a bad time, she said.

Sardines

Robert James Berry

We ate Portuguese sardines
and rye bread
the day my mother died
at home my aunt drank
two bottles of wine
and wept for her sister
my uncles jested in the pool.
When the sun set over your death
it was like a long blazing fanfare.

Dawn

Robert James Berry

I could write about
a whole field of potatoes
and the world wrapped
in a moon-white shawl
and the early crocuses
piercing the frosty ground
but I'd rather see dawn
fresh as pale apricots.

Two Faces of Posterity

in Chiado, Lisbon

Henry King

Tourists are queuing up to have their photo
taken beside the famous poet's statue,
but despite the attention paid to him
Pessoa looks inexorably grim:
he seems to ask himself whether more know him
from guide books than have ever read his poems.

Opposite him, more perfectly ignored
than homeless immigrants who line the road,
Antonio Ribeiro sits, face creased with laughter,
whom this part of the city is named after.

People Made Glasgow

Kate Tough

Shame in our hulls
why else would we drink to incoherence
jump on the heads of passing men
punch our women
tell our children in a checkout queue,
'Ah hate bank holidays cuz it means Ah huftae
look at yous fir three days no two.'

The whip's crack comes
a little after
the whip's stroke.

People Make Glasgow
obese, rotten-mouthed
stroke-felled, emphysemic
tumour-choked
aye, an proud ae it.
What we murdered them for
we kill ourselves with.

The whip's crack comes
a little after
the whip's stroke.

Brutalised Africans made Glasgow
amazing disgrace, how sweet the
civic amnesia...
mansions without plaques
unrevised street names
no memorial.
So, sign-up for the new city tour—

The Glasgow Merchant Experience!
Below deck on the Waverley
100 unclothed families
close-chained to plank beds
30 dead since it left Dunoon!
On the dock, a real live auction!
Feel the excitement as you bid for your very own slave!

Notes: William McDowall's plantation slaves were given Scottish names, such as, 'Glasgow'.

The 1779 folk hymn, Amazing Grace, was written by John Newton; former slave trader and slave-ship captain.

From the sequence *Returns of the Past*

Olive M Ritch

Fragment 1

a

cross

on the shore

left behind

f

o

r

m

e

someone is saying:

take the cross and follow me

Julianna Gee was born on Good Friday, and although she does not refer to the significance of the day she was born directly, she does use biblical iconography and allusion in her journal on many occasions.

Julianna, To Herself

I have had to learn
that eyes and ears
do their own doing
in the silence
between words
for something has happened –
my words slip, slide,
and slither; sometimes,
in the margins of thought,
words (right or wrong) insist,
persist, as if heavy waves
hitting the Yesnaby cliffs
need to be built again
in language – made real –
unreal; I cannot resist
translating the untranslatable –
the undone business (of words)
is my undoing and is what
I speak of, this morning,
the vast sea reaching out,
reaching out from my feet to   America

Fragments 20

every morning, I
begin my once upon
a time –

someone is saying:
go on, go on, you
must go on

Who is urging Julianna to keep going? Throughout her journal, she makes reference to 'someone is saying' and 'someone said', but her 'someone' does not have a name and in that sense never fully appears on the pages of her journal. Thus, we do not know whose voice is telling her to 'go on'. This is reminiscent of the question in T.S. Eliot's poem, *The Waste Land*: 'Who is the third that always walks beside you?' – a reference to the appearance of the risen Christ on the road to Emmaus, and the way in which he is not recognised, as if he is not fully present.[1] For Julianna, born on Good Friday, the significance of this passage can be understood in terms of the need to be told to keep on, keeping on, especially on the Saturday before the resurrection, when the world is without hope.

---

1 T. S. Eliot, *The Waste Land*, p. 73.

Fragments 23

Someone is saying:
Julianna is not herself today –
so, who am I?

Someone said: Julianna
is dead in her head

Someone is saying,
someone said:

The Disappeared

Who will forget Julianna
(the Julianna in happy pictures,
smoking a cigarette) – who will forget
the Julianna in a home
with no remembrance
of former things,
no remembrance
of things to come,
and who will forget
that voice saying: she's a burden,
a burden like the grasshopper in Ecclesiastes.

Fragment 49

no

more

w

o

r

d

s

only the mumbling pebbles in the darkness

Just Someone to Keep My House Clean

William Bonar

My flat has been well tended.
It gleams as if buffed

with a soft cloth.
It has nothing to do with me.

I am a hermit crab
who has found an abandoned

nautilus shell;
or once the heart of a great beast

its chambers
petrified with the ages,

still gleaming with the lustre
of a mighty life surge.

Reconstruction

Dave Hook

I wake up nothing but a pile of bones
Jigsaw puzzle spine, ribs like a xylophone
Skeletal scaffolding otherworldly and grey
Skinless finger spiders reacquaint ma skull with ma brain
I stretch ma ribs to cracking point to put my lungs in their cage
Ligaments creep and slowly cover ma frame
Along limbs, weeds grow and spread to function as veins
A ragged breath rasps and sets ma heart pumping again
Eyeballs hop into sockets where they fuse with ma optic nerves
Sheet lightening strikes on grey matter as ma thoughts disperse
Skin over jawbone, stubble on face
Mouth open wide, I reattach ma tongue in its place
One by one I push teeth into gums
Nails into fingers as air bleeds into lungs
After retrieving ma organs from canopic Jars, I regrow ma scars
All the while ma head aches like a broken heart

Sorry if I'm being kind of oblique
But there's a crack in ma skull that leaks punchlines in ma sleep
They trickle down ma face, drip, collect in a pool
And a form black shellac disc peppered with grooves
In the morning, the record player sucks it greedily in
Arm puts needle tae skin, inject: the machinery sings
It starts to sink in as the scenery swims
And if you're all sitting comfortably then we can begin

This is a daily reconstruction
I put the pieces back together but don't read the instructions
And sometimes there's parts left over when I'm done
I put them in a box and try not to think of them much

Then the Birds Came

MacGillivray

The birds
came in flocks, in June.
Some said it was omen, others angels –
still others devils. Only the fishermen breaking bread at
dawn, saw the strange winged beings dive-plummet
for the fish and rise again.
Egret, pippin-jay, swan, swallow,
nightingales, doves, flamingo,
wrens, ravens, crows, vultures,
blue-tits, red-tits, brown-tits,
kingfishers sparrows, plovers,
gulls of all kinds;
night gulls, herring gulls,
blackfoot gulls,
red winged gulls,
white winged gulls,
yellow billed gulls.
Hawks; penny hawks,
black hawks,
ruffed hawks,
gold hawks,
devil hawks,
warblers,
hummingbirds

…

the noise,
the noise
in the
dust.

Winter Fire

MacGillivray

I could taste the stars, planets too, mars in the mouth
anemone, graphite filings. Venus, not what you would think:
bitter that one – the guilt of stinging nettles that one, the
tongue swells. Jupiter: as if mint became a stone and was kept
in freezing flowing water for three days, split in half and
there was a seed inside. Mercury – swift! Silvered, yes. But
this one was different, this one; I woke in the night and I
turned to my wife.
As she gripped me she said, 'What's the matter, what is it?'
I said 'I've bitten my tongue in my sleep.'
She said 'salt water' I said 'no.'
'What do you mean?' she said.
I said 'I've bitten my tongue in my sleep because the taste of
this one was blood.'

Achram and his guns

Jenni Daiches

Achram from Afghanistan hunts deer in Knapdale.
In the early morning he leaves his lochside house
with guns and dogs. He translates well to Argyll's
hills. Perhaps his ancestors killed some of mine
when Scottish soldiers tramped his terrain and failed
to quell its wild tribesmen. Dorothy his wife
is English. No one tells them to go home.

Achram from Afghanistan is big and handsome.
In the early morning Arran's ragged mountains
perhaps cast sparks of Parvan. The loch rests peaceful
as the light returns, the water silent. His gun
gentle on his arm he follows deer tracks in the ground
soft under the trees. He seeks not vengeance,
but venison. His brother visits, impeccable in tweed.

In Memory of Alexander Hutchison 1

Richard Price

I first knew Sandy in the early 2000s, through I think the poets Peter McCarey and Gael Turnbull, friends in common. Sandy, like Peter and Gael, was coming from a different kind of modernism than the preachin' and a haranguin' (and life-stilling) of Eliot and Pound. Instead Sandy's emphasis on the joys and laughter of the body, of, especially, song, enfused a poetry that hit you from several glorious directions at once, very ancient like magic, then sophisticated, dense with thingicity (he would not have liked that word!) and dramatic all in a Renaissance way, and that joy in cheeky provocation. His poetry has not just a richness of vocabulary but a richness of social observation, a keen understanding of the mattedness of life (with a very naughty, comedic touch), and in his longer work there is a terrific rhythmic propulsion. Privately it is his emotional open-ness I loved, never afraid to love and to talk about love in all its variation, never afraid to share, put people in touch with each other and encourage and in poetry offer tactful well-judged advice. He once sung Burns's 'My Love is like a Red Red Rose' at a family Burns Supper I had in my home – his singing voice, as his speaking voice, had delicacy, poise, grace.

In Memory of Alexander Hutchison 2

Kathrine Sowerby

I'd heard him read and sing many times, waved him away from Tell it Slant when he stayed behind to wash glasses, but the memory of Sandy I hold close is in the breakfast room of his favourite B&B in St Andrews, early spring sunshine behind him. The mustard yellow walls covered in the owner's wildlife photography and a vase of pink tulips bending wildly in the middle of the table.

I was having a difficult time, had faffed about whether I could go to StAnza that year, and Sandy sat calmly eating the terrible porridge, asking me questions, talking about poetry, telling me about his family and the dads' group he belonged to, never intruding with his advice but gently offering solid paths to follow.

What I liked and appreciated about Sandy's counsel was the equality he handed to the expansive histories that interested him and his care of the small things too.

There are pink tulips on my table today and I hear Sandy's voice suggesting I pop a pin through the stems, keep them standing upright.

Bones and Breath

Alexander Hutchison

Here's me
barely out
of the nest,
my mouth

rinsed: shadow
and shape
astir on dusty
ground.

Heart brims
and spills.

Words try
eyes and wings;
try air.

The bones light,
my breath light.

Hueso y Respiro

Alexander Hutchison
from the collection *Gavia Stellata*, translated by *Juana Adcock*

Heme aquí
salido apenas
del nido;
mi boca

enjuagada: sombra
y forma
se agitan en polvo
en tierra.

Corazón al borde
se derrama.

Las palabras prueban
ojos y alas,
prueban aire.

Los huesos, luz;
respiro luz.

In Memory of Alexander Hutchison 3

Ellen McAteer

I first met Sandy at the Scottish Writer's Centre in 2010. Having just moved back to Glasgow after fifteen years away, I asked a table of members if there were any neglected contemporary Scottish writers I should read. Sandy, glass in hand, immediately replied 'Me!' I laughed, but when I began to read him I had to agree. His Scales Dog and Carbon Atom were stunningly original in both language and style, but not widely known. He told me he had taken up to 13 years between books in the past. I came to realise this was because he was a true craftsman. His best advice to me as a poet was 'Slow down.'

Shortly after moving back, I got a place on the Clydebuilt poetry apprenticeship scheme. The tutor turned out to be Sandy. By that time we had become regular partners in whiskey, poetry and song. He was an easy friend, but a hard master. When he introduced us at our Clydebuilt launch, he named us all as members of his crew. I was the cabin boy! It took me a while to appreciate what he was doing for me. Sandy forced me into a real apprenticeship. He made me take my time and work hard. When I did begin to have some success, he was a warm supporter. Through his works, I am still learning from him. A true makar.

In Memory of Alexander Hutchison 4

Cheryl Follon

Well, it starts with a happy face; kind and twinkly eyes. No snowman though, no Father Christmas. This guy chased an angry gypsy away with a ballad! There was someone I knew in the depths of despair – actually, way past that – and Sandy said, 'Let me talk to them.' I knew he could handle it, I knew he could make them better.

King of Mayhem. Nights in the Polish Club – round trays of vodka and beer (Sandy bought five rounds for everyone's two). So generous. Yes; infinite generosity, and what you call a bon vivant! A bottle of malt guzzled in a huddle – lots of things done in huddles, shared.

This tribute starts and ends with a happy face. Doesn't end.

Mr Scales Walks his Dog

Alexander Hutchison

The dog is so old dust flies out from its arse as it runs;
the dog is so old its tongue rattles in its mouth, its eyes
    were changed
in the 17th century, its legs are borrowed from a Louis
    Fourteen
bedside cabinet.
The dog is barking with an antique excitement.
Scales dog is so old its barks hang in the air like old socks,
    like faded paper flowers.
It is so old it played the doorman of the Atlantic Hotel
    in The Last Laugh,
so old it played the washroom attendant too.
Scales dog is so old he never learned to grow old
    gracefully.
Scales dog bites in stages.
Scales dog smells of naphtha.
Scales dog misjudges steps and trips.
Scales dog begs for scraps, licks plates.
Scales dog is seven times older than you think:
so he runs elliptically; so he cannot see spiders; so he is
    often distracted;
so he loses peanuts dropped at his feet; so he has suddenly
    become diabetic
and drinks from puddles; so there is bad wind in his
    system that came over
with the Mayflower; so he rolls on his back only once a
    week.
Scales dog is Gormenghast, is Nanny Slagg.
Scales dog is Horus, is Solomon Grundy.
His body makes disconnected music.

El Señor Balanza Pasea a Su Perro

Alexander Hutchison

from the collection *Gavia Stellata*, translated by *Juana Adcock*

El perro es tan viejo que le sale polvo a borbotones del culo
    cuando corre;
el perro es tan viejo que la lengua le traquetea en la boca,
sus ojos fueron cambiados
en el siglo XVII, sus patas son prestadas de una mesilla
    de noche
estilo Luis XIV.
El perro está ladrando con una emoción anticuaria.
El perro Balanza es tan viejo que sus ladridos se quedan
    colgados en el aire como calcetines viejos, como
    flores de papel desteñidas.
Es tan viejo que actuó en el papel de portero del Hotel
    Atlántico en El último,
tan viejo que actuó en el de mozo de baño también.
El perro Balanza es tan viejo que nunca aprendió a
    envejecer con gracia.
El perro Balanza muerde por etapas.
El perro Balanza huele a nafta.
El perro Balanza calcula mal el paso y se tropieza.
El perro Balanza pide las sobras, lame los platos.
El perro Balanza es siete veces más viejo de lo que crees:
así que corre en elipsis; así que no ve arañas; así que se
    distrae seguido;
así que se le pierden los cacahuates que le tiran al suelo;
    así que de pronto se ha vuelto diabético
y bebe de los charcos; así que tiene un mal aire en el
    sistema que llegó
con el Mayflower; así que se echa a rodar sólo una vez a
    la semana.
El perro Balanza es Gormenghast, es Nanny Slagg.
El perro Balanza es Horus, es Solomon Grundy.
Su cuerpo hace música inconexa.

He is so old his eyes are glazed with blood;
so old wonders have ceased; so old all his diseases are
    benign; so old
he disappoints instantly; so old his aim is bad.
Scales dog is so old each day Scales urges him to die.
Scales dog puts on a show like a bad magician.
Scales dog squats as if he was signing the Declaration of
    Independence.
Scales dog is so old worms tired of him.
So old his fleas have won prizes for longevity.
So old his dreams are on microfilm in the Museum of
    Modern Art.
So old he looks accusingly.
So old he scratches for fun.
Scales dog was buried with the Pharaohs, with the
    Aztecs; draws social
security from fourteen countries; travels with his blanket;
    throws up on
the rug; has a galaxy named after him; Scales dog runs
    scared;
would have each day the same, the same;
twitches in his sleep;
wheezes.

Es tan viejo que sus ojos están embetunados con sangre;
tan viejo que las maravillas han cesado; tan viejo que
    sus enfermedades son benignas; tan viejo
que al instante queda mal; tan viejo que su puntería es
    mala.
El perro Balanza es tan viejo que Balanza le suplica todos los
    días que se muera.
El perro Balanza hace teatro como un mal mago.
El perro Balanza se acuclilla como si firmara la
    Declaración de Independencia.
Tan viejo que los gusanos se hartaron de él.
Tan viejo que sus pulgas han ganado premios por
    longevidad.
Tan viejo que sus sueños están en microfilm en el Museo
    de Arte Moderno.
Tan viejo que mira acusador.
Tan viejo que rasca por placer.
El perro Balanza fue enterrado con los faraones, con los
    aztecas; recibe seguridad
social en catorce países; viaja con su manta; vomita en
el tapete; tiene una galaxia bautizada en nombre suyo; el
    perro Balanza corre asustado;
por él todos los días serían iguales, iguales;
pega respingos mientras duerme;
da resuellos.

In Memory of Alexander Hutchison 5

Hazel Frew

Alexander Hutchison changed my life, marked my poetic development. From the moment we met there was a spark of recognition, a sense of understanding. I loved his patient way of thinking and talking – never hurried, everything in its own time. His philosophy, to which I now subscribe: just keep pecking away. In other words keep working at it and it will come right – not always but enough to make a rule of it.

He lived effortlessly, seamlessly, with complete zen, seemed serenely happy in his own skin. Whether the swan's legs were whirling uncertainly beneath the surface, he never showed. He provided a level playing field, was reliable and steadfast, an absolute find of a friend.

Sandy filled the space of any company but never dominated, content to share his limelight. He had real presence and gravitas, a serious charm, along with a mischievous sense of humour – he loved to tell silly jokes in amongst the sober stuff.

We met in 1997, when I was 29 and he was 53, at a group called Wordshare in Glasgow. Wordshare was magical, the brain child of Alan Falconer, readings took place upstairs at the RAFA near Charing Cross. At that stage I had some work published in magazines but had never read in public. The calming candlelight made it easy to do. Sandy joined the group not long after I did and become a permanent fixture, an essential core. Having arrived back in Scotland from Canada he wanted to try out his singing voice and so we were treated to many ballads and songs, often accompanied by his friend and talented guitarist Michael Simons.

We met a few times a month, attended the Sunday Rhymes at Brel and any other poetry events we could get out to. We got ambitious, put on poetry and music nights at the Polish Club with the help of the poet Basia Palka. We had many celebrations there in Parkgrove Terrace, raised Zywiec, Zubrowka, Goldwasser and ate barszcz and homemade pierogi – made by a formidable Polish cook – had Christmas dinner, pulled crackers, laughed and sang.

Sandy was the backbone of the group and could always be relied upon to give an honest appraisal. He patiently read all my work, went through it with a fine-tooth comb, colourfully telling me exactly what he liked and didn't. He had a very clear idea of what was good, what would work. He helped endlessly with all my quirks, endorsing, legitimating.

He talked about the experience of writing 'Mr Scales' at the Auction and passed on copies of *Deep Tap Tree* and *The Moon Calf* to me. I was lucky enough to hear him read from these books many times. As the years passed I was privy to the unfolding of his talent, a poetry surpassing itself, becoming legendary, in its range, wisdom and humour. 'Carbon Atom', the brilliant 'Scales Dog', 'Bones and Breath', 'Tardigrade', 'Gavia Stellata.'

Sandy was very proud of his poetry, certainly knew his own worth. Forthright, he was no yes-man, no pillar of the establishment. He didn't suffer fools or bad poetry gladly. He voiced very colourful opinions, championed himself. He was formidable, fantastic.

Above all he was fun, youthful, playful. I can picture him ranging up and down the grassy slopes of Kelvingrove Park, as he did one summer evening before buying us a pot of sweet chilli mussels in Stravaigin – smacking his lips and saying, 'That was fine, let's order up another one.'

For a long time we planned a poetry road trip, imagined a convoy of poetry coaches trucking up to the highlands and on to the islands, our scarves flying in the breeze. That trip never happened, though we did make it to Shetland together, ate scallops in dank Voe stone. I remember him crowned with happiness over his success at wowing a tough Lerwick crowd with Peggy Gordon, waving him and Meg off at Orkney.

When Sandy won the Saltire Prize in 2014 I said, 'About bloody time!' He smiled and replied emphatically, 'No. The right time.' That was him to a T.

Alexander Hutchison did so much for me, woven in the warp and weft of my life, into the seasons, he was there for birthday parties, for celebrations, for advice, for good company, his face smiling in the audience of all my readings. He was there on some very bleak days too, to take my hand. He sang at my mother's funeral. It was an honour for me to give the eulogy at his.

The last time I saw him we had dinner at Ranjit's Kitchen on Pollockshaws Road with Meg and Cheryl Follon. Sandy was very ill but still shone and looked rosey cheeked in the soft light. He asked for Indian sweets and when given the bag, opened it, took out two pieces and insisted on giving the rest to me. I watched him, straight backed, walking with customary pride as he crossed the busy southside street, weaving his way through the traffic, his cap on his head. My last snapshot memory of him. He was my friend. I was the lucky one.

Everything

Alexander Hutchison

Everything is racing
   everything is vanishing

Everything is hosted
   everything is vanishing

Everything in the world that's seen
   everything is vanishing

All the angels rise and sing
   everything is vanishing

Everything that's clothed or bare
   everything is vanishing

Anything for a second there
   everything is vanishing

Everything is racing
   everything is vanishing

Everything is hosted
   everything is vanishing

Music, lovers, pillowslips
   everything is vanishing

Lightning, thunder, hail and rain
   everything is vanishing

In the mountains, on the streets
   everything is vanishing

Todo

Alexander Hutchison
from the collection *Gavia Stellata*, translated by *Juana Adcock*

Todo torrente
  todo disipándose

Todo amparado
  todo disipándose

Todo lo que se ve en el mundo
  todo disipándose

Los ángeles todos elevan su canto
  todo disipándose

Todo lo vestido o sin
  todo disipándose

Todo por un segundo ahí
  todo disipándose

Todo torrente
  todo disipándose

Todo amparado
  todo disipándose

Música, amantes, fundas de almohada
  todo disipándose

Relámpagos, truenos, granizo, y lluvia
  todo disipándose

En las montañas, en las calles
  todo disipándose

Scissors, paper, rock, hands
  everything is vanishing

Everything is racing
  everything is vanishing

Everything is hosted
  everything is vanishing

The fox at night, the birds aloft
  everything is vanishing

Speedwell, crocus, lotus, rose
  everything is vanishing

With arms spread wide
  everything is vanishing

With soft foot-fall
  everything is vanishing

Everything is racing
  everything is vanishing

Everything is hosted
  everything is vanishing

Hear it now, see me now
  everything is racing
    everything is vanishing

Love each other, love each other
  everything is hosted
    everything is vanishing

Tijera, piedra, papel, manos
   todo disipándose

Todo torrente
   todo disipándose

Todo amparado
   todo disipándose

El zorro en la noche, los pájaros en el aire
   todo disipándose

Verónica, loto, azafrán, rosa
   todo disipándose

A brazos abiertos
   todo disipándose

Con paso suave
   todo disipándose

Todo torrente
   todo disipándose

Todo amparado
   todo disipándose

Escucha ahora, mírame ahora
   todo torrente
      todo disipándose

Ámense unos a otros, ámense unos a otros
   todo amparado
      todo disipándose

In Memory of Alexander Hutchison 6

AB Jackson

In 2011 I was asked if I would like to be photographed in the nude for a charity calendar project, 'The Naked Muse', alongside eleven other male poets. I had no hesitation in declining. Having known Sandy for six years or so, however, I had a feeling it might just tickle him, and emailed him the details. A few months later, there he was: mister September, emerging in his birthday suit from a clump of bracken in the middle of some forest, arms akimbo, looking like a rather benevolent silverback. Needless to say, he was by far the oldest poet in the calendar, but it was entirely appropriate for him. He was in the thick of it, in the world, in the moment, having fun. He was only slightly concerned that he appeared to have the semblance of man-boobs, when in fact, he insisted, he didn't really.

The following year I was asked to contribute a poem to volume two of the Birdbook anthology series, edited by Kirsten Irving and Jon Stone at Sidekick Books. A list of birds was circulated in a Google document, and poets then bagged whatever one they fancied, first come first served. I passed on the details of the project to Sandy, in case there was anything he'd be interested in. When the book was published, it included his poem 'Gavia Stellata', one of his very best; so good, in fact, that it was included in the Forward Book of Poetry, and Sandy invited me down to the prizegiving event in the Queen Elizabeth Hall in September 2014. At that time, famous actors and broadcasters were hired to read out a selection of poems on stage – an approach which caused much controversy – and we sat through a rotation of readings by Cerys Mathews, Juliet Stevenson, Simon McBurney, and Samuel West. It was Samuel West who stepped forward and, to the packed hall of a thousand people, announced: "'Gavia Stellata' by Alexander Hutchison." I think we both jumped in our seats. As West read out the poem, I sneaked a look at Sandy's face: rapt in appreciation, a wee smile. It is among my happiest and proudest moments.

Alexander (Sandy) Hutchison
20th October 1943 – 22nd November 2015

The Gutter Interview: Darren McGarvey

Darren McGarvey is a writer, rapper, community arts leader, journalist and social commentator who goes by the name 'Loki.' To say that he attracts controversy and divides opinion would be an understatement. Having released seventeen albums, Loki is an established voice in the Scottish hip hop scene, and has, largely since the independence referendum, garnered a wider audience for both his music and his writing. He is currently working with Police Scotland and the Violence Reduction Unit, and sits on the Editorial Board of Bella Caledonia. His eighteenth album, Trigger Warning, is expected this year.

GUTTER: Let's talk a bit about the referendum, which is when most people first heard your voice. How did you get involved?

DM: I was about a week sober, and I went to a Yes Scotland office. I met with a perfectly nice woman, and I suggested some things. I thought it was just a place where you could go spitball ideas. So I went in and was like 'right okay, I think we should be having debates in schools, and I think we should take these to working class communities.' And she's just sitting there kind of like 'who the hell are you, this is a place where you come and print out flyers, and go and hand out flyers, there's a chain of command and what are you talking about?' You know what I mean? That's the feeling that I got. But I didn't really understand what that meant until later. She gave me an email address for National Collective and sent me on my way.

Anyway, that was my first instance, and then I wrote a piece and National Collective re-published it and declared me a member of National Collective, which was brilliant for me because I was like, here's someone trying to adopt me. I just feel like an outcast, and here is an official-looking thing, that looks all fancy. It looks like the bloody Guardian online this thing, you know, and they're saying I'm a member. I didn't tell them I was a member. I didn't sign a membership form. They obviously want me as part of what they're doing. These are artists. These are hard core artists. I've found my tribe. Completely misunderstood the whole thing, you know, completely.

And then my journey was eventually, closer to the referendum, going to a

Radical Independence meeting, talking at a couple RIC events, feeling a bit more at home there than I had at the NC events, where the awkwardness was hysterical. I mean, really hysterical. It was like a kind of mediocre Bob Dylan album, where everyone was just dead happy, and there was no sense of urgency or anger about the issues. So when I got up and started talking about poverty and child abuse and all that, they were just like *laughs* 'what the fuck are you?' Leading up to the referendum the relationship that I had with National Collective just kind of broke down. I had underestimated how closely aligned NC were to the mainstream Yes campaign and the SNP. There was no desire to create radical art. It was about giving the Yes movement a cultural feel. NC were very kind to me in the beginning and in many ways were victims of their own success. I was drawn in by the trouble maker rhetoric. I wanted a stake in how the group was running but was always held at arm's length because I happen to be a genuine trouble maker. With me it's not an image but I take responsibility for not reading the fine print. I just thought it ironic they couldn't facilitate democratic structures in their own ranks but were demanding democracy from afar. I wish them all well. We just have very different ideas about what political art looks and feels like.

GUTTER: So do you see yourself politically aligned to something in what you're writing now?

DM: Not really, I mean I just feel apprehensive about attaching to one thing now. See, it dawned on me just before the referendum that what we had done was just become the same as the side that we were trying to behave differently from. I think I became a bit nihilistic after that, once the dream was dead for me. The 'Yes' movement is not any more virtuous than what came before. It's more dangerous sometimes because elements of it can't see how they've been corrupted already. Political pragmatism has infected the public mind. Now we all see ourselves as movers and shakers when really we are foot soldiers and sound bite repeaters.

GUTTER: They believe they're the good guys.

DM: Aye. Cowboys and Indians. There's nothing more dangerous than that kind of moral certainty. I mean the 'Yes' movement is more patriarchal than folk will admit, and it was made up of wee micro-empires all with guys at the top of them, calling the shots, with no democratic accountability – all demanding democracy from someone else, but incapable of facilitating it in their own ranks. So if the power had came up here after the 'Yes' vote, it would have just went sideyways, and nobody would have wanted to talk about class because they'd have felt vindicated in winning the referendum by postponing that discussion.

So I feel I have more clarity and focus now. What I draw out is the absurdity of it, the moral posturing that goes on on both sides, the distortions. And also in a lot of what I write – I try to bring my own frailty and my own absurdity to the fore, as a starting point, to disarm anyone who might think I'm trying to be holier than thou. I'm absurd, that's my starting point. A lot of what I do is motivated by ulterior movies: prejudice, guilt, shame, all of these things. I think that that is all playing out on the stage of a public discourse except we're all giving ourselves a free pass to be inauthentic. But that's just my view.

GUTTER: Do you feel excluded? Do you think politics and the arts in Scotland in general doesn't have a space, or enough space , for someone like you?

DM: Space is opening up because social media kind of democratises things a wee bit. It's important to say as well that I don't think there's a malign intention behind the institutions that at this point are still overly packed with a people of a certain kind of background. I don't think there's anything malign about that. But I do think that social media has become a vehicle not only for other forms of culture, to have a platform and find an audience, but also to create the dialogue that needs to happen in order to get these institutions a bit more representative of the wider population.

You see there's a lot of positive progress that's happened in terms of representation for different minority groups in society. Whatever way you slice it. Progress is happening. But the one thing that falls to the bottom of the argument all the time is class and the background in which someone comes from. I think that class is the vehicle that distributes a lot of the other privilege. Progressivism makes class struggle more difficult as it cuts diagonally across everyone, placing them into sub-groups competing against each other to be heard.

Another thing worth mentioning is the fact that people from a high social class, who are better educated and so on and so forth, they have had an immense enabling and empowering effect on my life. They key to it has often been that, because they're not dealing with the chronic stress of poverty, they have the time and headspace to notice things about you that other people haven't had time to notice.

Then, if you are actually spending time around someone who comes from further up the food chain, you get an insight into how their emotional framework can absorb stress. You get to see how their lifestyle is conducive to peace of mind a wee bit more than the chaotic lifestyle I come from. So you get an insight. This is another reason why we should look for more opportunity to cross-pollinate these worlds.

Social movements, revolutionary movements often have a very scary, working class, battering ram aspect to it, but there is also a lot of expertise and stuff that comes from further up the food chain. It enables it. It enables it and brings a shape, and a signature to what could be interpreted as just chaotic anger. And sometimes that's how social movements progress. I think how society progresses, when people interface and mix.

GUTTER: But at the same time it can be a deeply patronising relationship, a middle class approach that's about improving working class people, about 'acceptable culture.'

DM: Aye, it's like Tom Leonard says

that about poetry. When he talks about how a lot of poetry came to be excluded. That when people write with that poetry voice, that kind of English poetry voice or British poetry voice, sorry. He says what that says about poetry is that it's this class structure being reinforced: if you don't learn this language you can't write poetry and that is the perfect metaphor for a lot of how society works in Britain.

I come from a working class background but I'm sitting here saying my life has benefited from interfacing with people who I would say are middle class or upper middle class, because I've had that experience. The reason that that experience empowered me was because they took me as I was, so they didn't ever try to tell me how to speak. They seemed just as interested in me as I was in them. That was the equaliser, you know, where, it's like you say, sometimes people go on out with an assumption that they know better. Because why wouldn't they? They live in a society that confirms them, that validates them all the time. Every form of culture available is from their perspective, so they would find it hard to imagine or relate to what it's like when you don't have that validation, when you're really unsure of yourself. Your brain has formed in such a way, because of the chronic stress of poverty, that the external world is not information; it's just noise and stress. It's hard to perceive how someone else might be interpreting life in such a stressful way, so all you're picking up is an attitude: 'I'm just trying to help them, why are they being so fucking angry, you know. Calm down.'

It's really difficult.

But, like I say, the social media aspect actually gives a platform to these different forms of expression, and over time we will hopefully develop a new approach and a new language for explaining these instances in which we lose each other in translation, speaking across the gulf of inequality.

GUTTER: You write most of articles in a more Standard English than you speak, whereas your lyrics are more close to your speech. What's that divide about to you?

DM: It's actually that I love Standard English as a form of rhetoric. Do you know what I mean by that? The written word in that form because it gives me a chance to show an aspect of myself that people might assume does not exist. So it's a way for me to say 'here, I can talk like you.' I can talk as well or better than you, with these tools, and I can rhyme in this language here, my native tongue, my colloquial expression, whatever you want to call it. I quite like it, and also I'm quite inspired by orators, who I don't always necessarily agree with, but I find them interesting because I see them going against things that no one else has went against, and I want to know how do they emotionally cope when everyone around them is saying, like they said to Christopher Hitchens, 'you can't go after Mother Theresa, what the fuck is wrong with you?'

I realise a lot of this game in public life is about sounding smart, it's not about being smart. Certainly, it's not about being smart. You know yourself, some of the muppets that are walking around out there, who sound clever. Oratory in this world is real power. It's real power, to affect emotionally, because nobody's interested in the data. Nobody wants to hear the facts. People are moved by emotional appeals to their sensibilities, to their identities. That's just a sad fact. So if that's the world we're living in, then I'm honing my skills for that environment.

This sort of difference between writing Standard English for journalism is simply that I have two different audiences. Increasingly, I can bring them together in conversation. My Twitter is mainly followed by other culture whores like me, who are selling a point of view, right? On Facebook it's totally different. So on Facebook, I share video content because video content insists on itself less, so someone can have it on in the background, on the train, on the bus. On Twitter I publish short-form articles, opinion pieces, long-form articles. I mean, there's no structure to some of this stuff that I write, and actually people seem to go for that, because they're so used to reading standardised, structured journalism, and they find that my stuff has a different rhythm to it, it's more lyrical, and it's refreshing.

GUTTER: With those two audiences, do you think you're trying to achieve something different – are you saying there's a hip hop audience and that's a similar audience to your videos, and there's a cultural audience that's interested in your political commentary?

DM: Actually, there's the hip hop

thing which is kind of almost separate from it. The Facebook following and the Facebook interaction seems to be driven by people who normally wouldn't comment on some of the national conversations that are going on. You notice on social media, you can tell from interactions who engages with what sort of stuff, and who doesn't.

For example, when I'd done a video after the fire in the Art School, and it was me saying 'why isn't my school as important as the Art School?' The reason I'd done that video was just because I was trying to articulate a feeling that is out there in housing schemes, where they look at their telly and they think, it's that thing again that I've not heard of and that I'm not interested in, why are they so sad about that burning down? Things burn down around here all the time. I was just trying to find an expression of that, and what I noticed was the video got thousands of views, but the only people who commented mostly were people who were against what I said. It was people usually who had some sort of emotional attachment to the Art School or had been to the Art School or had recognised its purpose and its influence on their life. So it's completely natural for them to watch this video and comment on it.

But the vast majority of views were generated by people who quietly agreed with it. You know how women say they don't feel as confident engaging in social media and arguments as men do, and there's evidence to support that? It's also the same for people who come from lower classes, I think a lot of the time, depending on who else is in the discussion. An example of that: I've never been to a Bella Caledonia editorial meeting even though I'm on the board. The idea of going to it fills me with anxiety. I've met most of them in person, but I just wouldn't put myself around a table because I would feel too self-conscious. That's a real thing. It's no one at that table's fault.

GUTTER: Do you see a big divide between your private persona and your public persona? Do you think that to some extent you're putting on a character?

DM: I have no control. I'm only now starting to get a sense of what people may think. I remember a time when I could publish an article and track its progress on all the platforms it was published on and engage in all the conversations that were going on about it. I don't do that now. I don't even know what's going on, so there's an element of resenting the fact you can't control what people think. But obviously consciously I do enjoy the fact that people will make assumptions about why I do certain things, because I enjoy seeing how wrong they are. For a lot of what I write, people say I'm some kind of Rise lackey. They think I'm part of a conspiracy to propagate Rise politics and fight the SNP. When I'm not. I'm sharing Rise articles, and I'm thinking, maybe someday soon I'll trust this movement the way I trusted the movement that came before. Maybe soon I'll be ready to trust it. For many people, the whole experience of socialism in Scotland in the last ten years was a complete fucking let down. To the point where we all turned to the SNP, but

without really looking, closely, at what they really were.

I annoy the Nationalists or Tories or Socialists or whoever might sit and go 'ach, that's just Loki, being Loki, writing this because such and such,' and they don't really know my motives. There's a performance aspect to a lot of this stuff that I write that they don't assume because they've only interfaced or seen me in a certain capacity. So they don't know that Andy Kauffman is a big influence for me, and his whole thing was about creating discord to see how people would react, throwing the cat among the pigeons. Poke the hornet's nest with a stick, for sport, you know? There is an aspect that I do enjoy about that, especially in such an uncertain time. It means that I can be unsure but still active because I go at each thing dead conscious about what I'm trying to achieve with it, but it doesn't necessarily mean it has to be part of a big consistent belief system. The referendum completely fractured me in terms of what I believe and what I want.

GUTTER: With those provocations, what response do you think you're after?

DM: My instinct seems to pull me toward talking about an absurdity of things. It seems to pull me toward challenging where the real power is in Scotland. Now I know that the power up here is eclipsed by the power of the government in London, but I'm coming from a school of thought that says 'power is always the problem.' And while I completely understand the rationale and pragmatism of people who would seize power to do with it things that need to be done, there also has to be attack dogs all the time, looking at that, and talking about that. Because there is a shelf life for how long you can have power before you become The Arsehole. I think some people in some parties are really getting close to that line. I believe it's an act of love to criticise the SNP and the Scottish government. You see that Rise irritate the SNP on the grassroots level and online. They irritate it. Which is exactly what radicals are supposed to do. They're supposed to keep the other people honest, just honest enough to make them tolerable. It's a fascinating time.

If it was me, I wouldn't be coming up with thinly veiled attacks on the SNP, which is what Rise is doing because they want to appeal to the disillusioned SNP member who might defect. I'd be setting my stall out more aggressively. I'd be calling bullshit everyday. I'd be developing a brand that has a bit more of a character to it, and not a kind of alternative take on this standard political brand, something that has a bit more character, a bit like what the Yes Campaign had, but something that is more true to Rise and not something that's not just manufactured to appeal to fucking everybody and their granny. Because Rise is not going to be a popular movement. Not to say that it won't be in the future, economic circumstances might demand socialism in its rawest form, but just now, people are more interested in having lower taxes draped in comforting social justice rhetoric that makes them feel as if they live in a fair country. The wheesht for

indy movement is hiding behind a need for pragmatism and using it as an excuse to take almost zero meaningful action on the fundamental issue facing Scotland: structural poverty. You need a radical movement that is relentlessly calling out that bullshit, every social media platform, every single day, repeating that message over and over. Taking the way Stuart Campbell does for Wings Over Scotland, I mean he shreds opposition at the gates for the SNP and he's not even on the payroll, he probably doesn't even speak to people in the high echelons of the SNP. This is now a functioning fucking cultural framework that protects and shuts down discussion while also imbuing soundbites and data and information for the general population to absorb and repeat to each other, so it's like a machine. Wings took Kezia Dugdale's quite ballsy idea to raise taxes and fucking treated it with a level of disdain that it's now actually being called the Better Together Tax. If you want to fight the SNP you need to fucking be original and you need to be really social media savvy.

People hate the union so much, and they hate Westminster, and they hate Labour so much that they're letting that prevent them from seeing any good ideas or any benefits that might come out of these institutions or political figures. I think that is dangerous because it means division becomes cognitive, you just dismiss the opposition; there's no free exchange of ideas when that stuff's going on. You've got all the SNP voters holding the line as well as the politicians. There's just this consistency, this monolith of opinion that just can't actually in realistic terms be competed with. The minute that you speak against it, you're actually surrounded online.

GUTTER: Yeah, that's a hundred thousand Malcom Tuckers.

DM: The only way to compete with that is to grow in capacity and to be sharper and wittier. Treat them with twice the ridicule that they're treating you, outflank them, outsmart them, out-joke them, out-blog them. It's the only way, or else we're looking at another fucking fifteen years of this, and that's pretty serious.

Let me qualify this by saying, a guilty pleasure of mine is being a passive observer, watching ruthless political people doing their business, right? I'm fascinated by the New Labour project, fascinated by how it took Thatcherism and just rebranded it, and made some modifications with the comfort and social justice rhetoric. This appealed broadly and got the power that they so needed to make the changes that they made. The SNP are a response to that reality but not so much a response in the sense of let's do something different, what they've done is, they've taken all the lessons from that sort of politics and they've turned the dial up in the social media age. They're the only institution, party, whatever you want to call it, equipped to navigate this new terrain, so they set the agenda. That's it.

There are many other things to bear in mind in terms of positives of the SNP. They've got a core principle that they've never ever budged on: independence. Never budged on it. Never will budge on it. That's a powerful thing for people who are looking to see evidence of virtue in politics, and it's actually something you can't remove from the SNP. It's fundamental, it's like tearing their heart out. You've got that aspect of it, and then in terms of actually improving access, particularly for women to take up position in politics and more fairly reflect the population that they serve, no one's done more than the SNP. So these are all massive strides forward.

GUTTER: Yeah, Thatcher really got rid of the idea of Conservatives being conservative. Blair destroyed the idea of Labour being socialist, but no one can stop the SNP from being nationalists.

DM: Aye, that's it. People will say, we'd never budge until it's independent. It means everything else around them can change. I think David Torrance wrote about this in his book, or an extra chapter in his book about the 'Yes' movement; of the SNP very much being created in the mold of Salmond: gregarious, cocky, dismissive of criticism, contemptuous of dissent.

Sturgeon's dealing with that hangover. It's not necessarily the SNP she would have created. She's just been waiting for her shot. She has a lot of amazing qualities as a leader, but she'll be doing things that would have been unthinkable to her earlier in her journey. Seizing power does mental things to people, changes their views and their outlook. She still retains a lot of things that people like about her, I think she's more popular now as a first minister than she was in her early days in the SNP when people were really irritated by her, saw her as a sort of Salmond drone.

They've got a lot of other skilful

politicians as well. Let's not underestimate the fact that the people who vote for them genuinely believe they are competent in government. It means that they are looking for something different in their government than what I'm looking for. I'm always moving around the public sector, and I'm faced with the police and I'm faced with the local authorities, and I'm faced with further education. I don't see competence in government. I see a rebranding exercise going on, where everything has the word Scotland put after it and has money pulled out of it. This aggressive centralisation where there's a tier of managers, there's a buffer between poorly managed institutions and accountable politicians. That's what's actually going on. People think that's good government?

GUTTER: Talking about the police then. Will you tell us a bit about what you've been doing with the Violence Reduction Unit? And are all cops still bastards or not?

DM: First of all, that's Louie from Hector Bizerk who says that, and Louie comes from a bit of a different kind of background from me. It's been brilliant. I took the idea to the VRU. I saw it as an opportunity to legitimise what I was doing at a time in my life where I've got to advance in some way. I saw it as an opportunity to take the next stage in my journey as a writer and work to a brief set by someone else and show that I can work among people and that I'm not always rabid. That was my motivation for doing it.

Since I've started, it's been interesting. Some of the actual work

that I've done, I'm working pretty much nonstop on a piece of art that will be published around domestic abuse. It will be a short film, a rap that features actors depicting a domestic abuse scenario from the perpetrator's perspective. And I've written lyrics and a vocal that go with it. Andrew MacKenzie's filmed it and directed it. Mick MacNeil, formerly of the Simple Minds, has played piano on it. I don't want to give too much away, but it's not a standard hip hop affair. We decided to go for a more classical vibe. We used *A Clockwork Orange* as a kind of reference point, ultra-violence being back-dropped with this classical sublime music, and also we thought that would be a way to avoid us falling into any clichés because there are a lot of clichés around these issues and there's a lot of clichés around how hip hop handles these issues. That's been ongoing. I've also done appearances and workshops in schools. I was in Low Moss Prison yesterday. I carry out other tasks on behalf of other branches. They all have access to me if they want me to do something for them. That's been good.

In terms of some of the pressures of it: I never felt under pressure from any exposure in the media before, I never felt scared for people to know certain things, but obviously when you're working on behalf of an organisation, particularly one as scrutinised as the police, then that brings with it different pressures because you have to put everything that you say through a filter. I'm lucky that there are no restrictions placed on me for what I can say apart from very obvious things, don't comment on issues that aren't to do with your role. Which I would have expected, you know what I mean?

I don't find it restrictive; though I have found there's a wee bit more pressure. When you do an interview for, let's say, the *Guardian* or *The Times*, not the *Evening Times*, in the time between doing the interview and it coming out I'm a lot more anxious and nervous because I have no control and I don't know what they're going to say. What are they going to write about? Have I slipped up? Have I said something? Did I criticise the government? Because you never know. That's based on my own paranoia. I'm usually free to say whatever I like. Also, journalists have a legitimate reason to scrutinise me more. So they can look at my past. For example, I had an ongoing charge from my relapse that was for a minor offence, and I mentioned this in an interview, not thinking anything of it, and that became the thing that all the other press asked me about. But this was a really difficult part of my life, and I've got other employers, and other things, all depending on people knowing I'm not a fucking mad criminal.

There is massive anti-police sentiment in working class communities, never mind the hip hop community. My true feeling is that a lot of the sentiment is cultural and doesn't always reflect the role that police have in communities, where they're first responders for wife beaters, for child abusers, they're first responders for people getting stabbed, they're first responders for so many things that we citizens turn a blind eye to or wouldn't deal with because it's not our problem unless

it happens to us. That's important to say. What people are skeptical of is the power that the police have as an institution. Anytime when people in schemes are trying to do something they shouldn't be doing, a police officers always there to fucking stop them from doing it.

What the public might not know, or might not get a sense of, is that the internal conversations that go on within these institutions often reflect the same concerns the public have. That's the same in journalism, that's the same in the local authorities everywhere. The people that work in these institutions are aware of these problems. They as individuals, or as wee cohorts, are always trying to advance that within mammoth institutions that have just been changed and amalgamated. It's an immense task influencing how a public institution behaves. That's something I've been challenged by because there was a time when I would have took a view not dissimilar to 'all cops are bastards.' If you're gonna say all cops are bastards, you just need to say all people are bastards, which is a far more accurate thing to say because the cops represent a cross section of people. If we want to affect how the police behave, it's no the police we need to deal with, it's the government we need to deal with, it's the law makers, the police are just enforcing that.

It's been a good experience working with the VRU. I hope they'll extend the contract. I've got six months; hopefully they'll extend it to a year. I'm just looking forward to actually publishing the art. I've done a lot of writing for them, but

I'm looking forward to publishing the art. Basically, my first brief was, write a rap around domestic violence. I said, I want to do it from the perpetrator's perspective, that'll be interesting, that'll be provocative. Something that we haven't seen. They were up for that. They didn't set me too many restrictions, and then I just went about it. It's capturing the thoughts of an abuser or perpetrator of domestic violence from the remorse stage through the tension stage to the moment before the explosive stage. A lot of the self-justification that goes on, a lot of the delusion that goes on, the victimhood that goes on in the mind of the abuser. What I'm trying to do is show that the behaviour we see objectively as controlling and dominating behaviour, where we assume intention, is actually rooted in victimhood, a delusional victimhood, and feeling completely besieged by this woman who dominates the man's emotions, because the man has no self-esteem. So he takes preventative measures to protect himself from emotional discomfort, and those measures are controlling, dominating, and abusive. But he doesn't see that until a wake up moment usually, unfortunately, an explosive act of violence.

[DM gets a phone call from his partner. Gutter asks about the baby, due 12 March]

DM: I realise it's controversial, and I realise because I'm very aware of different strains of feminism in Scotland and different modes of opinion on the issue,

I'm aware that some will be more accepting of this portrayal than others.

The important thing has to be that everybody understands the intention behind it: it's definitely not about making excuses for an abuser. It's definitely not about saying in any instance whatsoever that there's ever any excuse for a man, or anybody else for that matter, to be violent in the home or anywhere else. Definitely not. It's simply about trying to get to some of the more complicated emotional truths behind abuse.

We have a justice system that clamps down hard on it, that's evolved to deal with different types of abuse, and interface with it at different points in the cycle. We're quite advanced in that sense, which is good because the figures are rising. What I'm doing represents a tiny devotion of resources to exploring the issue in another way. It's not like we're saying the artist is going to solve domestic abuse, it's not for that at all. It's primarily about raising awareness of the issue among young people who normally wouldn't engage. It's about creating a piece of art that someone can watch and decide in the privacy of their own mind, am I on this spectrum? Can they self-identify, without having to say it to a pal, without having to admit it to anyone else?

If they get a wee tiny bit of insight that they might be developing bad habits, then they might pull themselves back from the cliff edge. This is true of all other forms of delusion, including addiction. It's a complicated process getting it finished because there's a lot of back and forth.

Taking great care that anyone watches it knows we are saying domestic abuse is wrong, no question.

GUTTER: Are you anxious about that response then?

DM: Slightly. However, I've managed to workshop it a couple times with women, young women, older women, women who are advocates in some capacity or another on behalf of other women. If I'm there, it gives the thing context. So the danger is when it's just in the public sphere and people are just taking it on its own merits without me selling it. How do we change it in such a way that gives it a wee bit more context? That's why it's taking its time. Also, each time we go through it, it gets better. It will be original, it will be provocative and something that can also be used as a tool in schools and prisons. Being tasked to write something that's supposed to function in all these different capacities is extremely challenging. But worth it.

GUTTER: Have you been looking at other writing about violence and domestic violence?

DM: I did a lot of research, mostly academic stuff during my research period before I submitted the first draft. I learned about the dissociative language that we use as people. We say, 'I lost the plot.' That's a way of disassociating from the responsibility of your own emotional management. In the context of domestic violence, this leaves a trail of delusion that leads straight to the abusive mind. The abuser followers a certain type of pattern that might find expression in different ways but when you get to the

core of it, it's a gathering snow ball of different ways to control the outcome of how the other person behaves. The song's called 'Gaslight,' making reference to the phenomenon named after the 1944 film, when you're gas-lighting, your actions are making your partner feel like they're insane and mentally disorientated, and in that disorientation you're manipulating them. So you're basically breaking them down until they think they're going off their nut, and then you present yourself as a solution. That was one of the most useful things that I found out.

In terms of research, I spoke to a social worker, I spoke to perpetrators, of all different kind of gradients. The former perpetrator that's turned their life around, that no longer engages in this stuff and can actually be open about what happened and what drove it. And then other men who haven't quite got that insight yet. Learning that there's not one profile for it. Which is why the piece became so long. I was trying to plant within the piece as much stuff as possible that other people watching it could identify with. There are references to social media, then there are more subtle references to – there's a line in it, 'the radiator's still warm, so you're no long oot. You've left your laptop on Facebook, and you've no logged oot.' So taking great care to try and plant lots of things were people can go 'oh, that's me, I can relate to putting my haun on the radiator and that being the measure of how long she's been away.'

The meeting with the social worker was extremely useful because it gave me an insight into the scale of the problem. I thought she was a social worker specifically tasked to deal with domestic abusers. It turns out, she's a social worker tasked to deal with everything, and it just so happens domestic violence is the things she always has to deal with because that's what's always happening.

This is a strange time for men who don't have a language to express disorientation. It's a controversial thing to say, but it's important that we're mindful of this as we advance the causes of minority groups because ultimately, with the collapse of industry, the young male has no sense of purpose beyond their daily impulses, and when you take away the traditional modes of masculinity and don't replace it with anything, then men just become a gaggle of consumer habits, with a big hole in the centre.

We must make sure we are trying to initiate young men into the wider conversation going on about their role in the modern society. I think the left are missing a trick on this – young men, feeling shut out of progressive conversations that increasingly dismiss and vilify them, are turning to You Tube, and they're typing in the words 'feminism', 'political correctness' and a whole pantheon of right-wing populists are waiting there with intellectual arguments as to why some feminists can't be trusted. Intellectual arguments as to why some ethnic minorities will engage in criminality more than others. The appeal of these people is not misogyny or patriarchy or racism. The appeal of these people is the veneer of reason many of them wear, arguably to mask their own

prejudices. This is something we have to understand on the left, because so much of our politics is driven by principle. But we increasingly feed into an irrational outrage culture to push our agenda and lose sight of the fact we are getting worse at making strong arguments for our positions.

People feel excluded from that conversation or haven't learned the trendy language to express or engage in it, they feel sometimes shut oot and shut down. You Tube's becoming a bit of a ghetto for it. These cultural libertarian guys are really clever and we need to tool up with something other than 'no-platforming' to compete with them. There's a few I can even name, Stephan Molyneux, Sargon of Akkad and Thunderfoot. Then there's Milo Yiannopoulos, who lefties would see as a weird, gay-hating, conservative, homosexual misogynist, but on the other he's backing up everything he says with data and making radical feminists look out of their depth of national TV – feeding the myth all feminists are mental. 'Actually the pay gap is not what it's made out to be, and here's why blah-blah-blah. Here's data that shows men are abused more online than women.' We need to answer people like him intelligently and with more respect because ultimately they represent lots of other people. We can't debate it by saying 'let's shut him down.' We can't debate it by saying, 'sign our petition that bans him from talking,' because that is an initiation of force in other people's eyes. Then they say, look at these loonies. They're trying to shut us down for having a different point of view. That's where men are turning in their confusion because we are punishing them for thinking out loud and not saying the right thing. I don't want men to turn there. We need to re-initiate them into our tribe or they'll come back and burn the whole village down. That means going to where they are even if we disagree.

GUTTER: The danger of what you're saying is that it's about speaking up for white men, which is a position that the left and the successes of feminism have rightly made very difficult.

DM: I think that's quite fundamental. One of the aspects of feminism that I find difficult, and I think a lot of feminists do, I certainly know some do that might not say it, but they are feminists: the whole position of the third wave radical feminists who super impose social theory onto everyone, so every single interface between people becomes a power dynamic. So why can't they grapple with an argument about class? Which is the original social theory. That is no way to challenge privilege. I'm aware of my privilege as a man. I'm aware of my privilege as someone who is not immensely well educated but someone who has now lived a lot and is able to talk well.

What we are witnessing just now is how debate suffers when we don't come out of our own narrow conversations.

GUTTER: I think privilege is a really useful concept to discuss, but here you're getting into a difficult idea of a hierarchy of privileges.

DM: I was trying to write about this a couple weeks ago. Is a black man from a lower class background more privileged than a white woman from an upper middle class background? There's so much subjectivity around the issue, it's actually dangerous. It's dangerous because a lot of how the progressive cause has advanced at the minute is force. It's the force of: 'you don't want to be associated with this misogyny do you? Well you better fucking adopt our position, and we're forcing this through.'

There's a fine line between direct action or activism and what's happening now, which is just a whole lot of stuff on social media, which gives off a whole different feel. People are judging feminism based on how social media feels, which is not quite accurate either. I don't know how you would go about it. I certainly wouldn't fucking nominate myself to chair such a discussion, but I think we need to try and find a way of engaging the points of view we disagree with more because we have so many enemies now.

You look around you, outside the echo chamber, everybody's a wee bit over here on the right. We need to go, okay, maybe you're not a misogynist just because you said this. Maybe you're not racist just because you said this. What is the pathology behind these points of view? I'm not saying give people a free pass, I'm just saying I can see there's a slow exodus over to the fucking dark side.

You can see the appeal of someone on the right who's not only wearing a veneer of reason, they're saying 'see all those imperfections you have, see all those times you open your mouth that make people around the table feel awkward, all those restrictions you feel placed on your speech, you don't have to worry about them over here. We accept you're human. We accept it's a crazy time to be alive, and that not everybody is a pure up-to-speed radical activist.'

That's the appeal, for a quiet life. How do we adjust to that reality? It's a crazy time. I have sat for many years reflecting on how much of my instinctive query of certain feminism is to do with honest inquiry and how much of it is to do with innate misogyny that might be a blind spot; because I'm misogynistic as any man or woman in a male-dominated society. It's original sin, you're kind of born with some degree of what we would nowadays call misogyny. That's a journey I've been on and continue to be on. I have women in my life that challenge me on things that I say and things that I think. That's important for me to say. For any man or woman who might be thinking, Loki sometimes he seems like a bit of a misogynist, did he not hate his ma? Everybody has these things. If that excludes me from engaging, then everyone has something that excludes them from engaging. Everyone's been shit to a partner, everyone's manipulated the opposite sex, everyone's took advantage of someone, everyone's laughed at a racist joke, and everyone's done all these things. We have a Left just now that is kind of detached from that truth about human frailty. It's about adopting an inauthentic persona and then signalling to people that you're a part of a collective – all in the name of empowering the individual apparently.

If Memory Serves, by Prof Herman Brown, BA, MA, PhD, FRHistS

Robin Jones

The deafness I suffer in my right ear is not a result of genetic mishap but, rather, a disability that I owe to what my parents, while they were still alive, referred to as a childhood accident. Let me here correct this historical injustice: I owe my deafness to a childhood *incident*.

It is a historian's[1] keenly felt responsibility that he stamp out euphemism wherever he finds it and there can be no doubt that 'accident' is, in this case, a particularly scandalous example of that shameful linguistic phenomenon. The evidence, dear reader, is unequivocal: it was no 'accident' at all.

***

When I was in my early teens my Father was a lay preacher[2] for the Church of Scotland; a duty he performed with all the earnestness the position demands. As such, he rightly believed that it was not only incumbent upon those so entrusted by God to sermonise Christian virtues but, wherever possible, to reify those virtues by one's own actions.

Now, when I was a young man my Father thought me, for one reason or the other, a little lacking in self-discipline. The solution – around my thirteenth birthday if I remember correctly – was what my Father described as 'a long-overdue introduction to adult responsibilities'. He resolved, to my then-great distress (though I now realise, of course, its necessity), that this would be best accomplished by my doing as he himself had done when he was my age, namely, by undertaking summer work as a farm hand. His cousin, Harris McGee, had a small dairy farm not far from Pitlochry. This, naturally enough, was to be my destination.

My visit to the McGee dairy was not a success, the work being, as it was, of little interest to me. I was not, it seems, blessed with a constitution that responds well to

---

[1] I am, first and foremost, a literary historian, my area of specialisation being the aesthetic theorists that emerged from the October Revolution.

Beyond the history of literary theory, my academic interests include, among others: occasional translation (I have recently received funding to undertake a rendering of The Brothers Karamazov into Scots); the life and works of Thomas Paine (of whom I am something of a minor biographer); and an amateur interest in experimental poetry (I am the editor of a pamphlet, now in its third issue, that combines 'found' poetry with avant-garde graphic design).

[2] A position in the Kirk more correctly known as a 'reader.' I have reluctantly included the more familiar term 'lay preacher' for fear of being misunderstood by less careful readers.

manual labour. Despite never trying to shirk work – unlike the other farm hands – I did, however, indulge in the farm's second most popular activity: trying to impress my second cousin Lotti (then thirteen years old). In accordance with pubescent tradition this was best achieved by performing any feat of stupidity or pointless exhibition of strength that opportunity afforded.

One of the most common – and overtly risky – rituals was the refusal to mount the tractor's trailer until it was moving at quite some speed. It was also, I need not add, one that my teenage vanity therefore obliged me to master. Unfortunately, it was a practice my Father had witnessed by chance when he delivered me at the start of that summer and had expressly forbidden me to perform. This restriction he had asked his cousin, Harris, to enforce. This, needless to say, presented me with something of a problem.

I was at least three or four years the junior of the other farm hands and felt the discrepancy keenly; never more so than when I was instructed to mount the trailer, to sit down and to find a secure spot before we pulled off. From my safe perch on the wheel arch I then had to watch while all the other boys leisurely finished their cigarettes, feigning absent-mindedness to Lotti while the tractor pulled away. Of course, before we got too far the boys would chase after us and – running alongside the trailer at no little speed – would swing themselves expertly up. From this proud coign of vantage they could then casually light another cigarette and half smile to/half ignore Lotti who waited in the farm house doorway until we were out of sight, wiping her hands on her apron.

I always fancied, in those moments as they settled into the trailer, that they smirked at me while I sat princely atop a bale or other such cargo. I still burn at the thought of it. There I was, a delicate school fellow whose mother had written to the teacher exempting her sickly child from Games, while the others sat round me, festering on the brink of manhood. Needless to say, it was an embarrassment that I could not allow to continue past the third week.

***

For the duration of my time at the dairy we each day lunched together in the kitchen of the farm house: Harris, his wife, Lotti, the farm hands and me. And everyday, as soon as lunch was over, the boys would excuse themselves and head out of doors where they could sit sunning in the yard, waiting for the farmer to finish his ale and cheese.

Before long he would emerge from the kitchen, light a cigarette, climb onto the tractor and, usually with a spit, start the engine. Invariably (though each day I prayed he would forget), Harris waited for me to climb aboard before he set off. Any delay on my part was rewarded with a choice phrase of agrarian language, new to my then-virgin ears. I soon learned not to keep him waiting.

And so the daily routine progressed those three first weeks, until one particular afternoon I resolved, *no more*; I was there to become a man, and a man I would become. I would come of age, and I would wait, like the others, until the trailer had moved off. The farmer's imprecations be damned.

The decision was not one I took lightly; after all, my Father had forbidden the practice. The choice, however, had been taken out of my hands.

I had, you see, been particularly violently belittled that morning by the 'older' boys for my (comparative) lack of sexual experience and I was determined – indeed I was steadfast – to establish equal standing in the group. It was, therefore, for this reason that that particular day after lunch, when the engine started, I stayed firmly where I was.

I should have anticipated, however, that my absence from the trailer would be noticed (indeed, there had never been a day before when it had not). I *should have*, dear reader, but I did not. And so, predictably, in starting the engine, my Father's cousin turned round, scowled at the empty trailer and barked at me something I am reluctant here to commit to the page. His tone was such that, despite my resolve to wait with the others, I involuntarily jumped up and jogged sheepishly towards the trailer.

Just as I did so, however, Lotti came out of the farmhouse door wiping her hands. The sight of the object of my pubescent desire filled me with a shame stronger in its effect than any malediction from the farmer. To call it a decision would be misleading: fate seemed to conquer free will.

Reaching the tractor I realised I was unprepared to climb aboard: my very spirit forbade it. With the quick thinking of difficult circumstance I banged my hands on the bed of the trailer mimicking footsteps; my heart beating with each false footfall. I stopped, already somewhat in awe of my own boldness, and waited to see if the effect was successful. To my delight and astonishment the tractor's engine roared and the trailer started moving away.

At this, I turned round to the other boys who appeared, it seemed to me, rather incurious for having witnessed such a *coup de maître* and gave them a conspiratorial wink. Seeing Lotti still looking on, I treated her to one of the same.

Then, in what seemed an instant, the boys threw away their cigarette butts and ran past me after the trailer. Resolving to do the same, I flashed my most charming smile at the lovely Lotti, who was still looking on from the doorway, and turned and ran after the boys, my breast swelling with adult pride.

To my surprise, however, upon turning around, I found the trailer already some distance from the farmhouse. To my even greater surprise the boys were already running alongside and clambering on.

Now, I hope I do not commit an immodesty if I reveal that mine is a family in possession of dependable legs and sturdy lungs: we have for a number of generations had a deserved reputation for being accomplished club runners, especially over the middle distances. The run ahead did not, therefore, strike me as overly daunting. Indeed, I clearly remember thinking, perhaps a little hubristically, that such a distance only afforded me the opportunity to prove myself the better. I was not, in my defence, altogether wrong.

Before long I had caught up with the trailer and was running alongside with enough ease to salute the farm hands as nonchalantly as I could manage. 'Alright, lads' was, I fear, the cretinous greeting. It was the first time I had risked such an overt informality with anyone on the farm (despite such modes of address being commonplace among the other boys). As it turned out, I was never to have the opportunity of repeating it.

I was still running along quite comfortably, eyeing the foot plate which ran along the back of the trailer in order to make my mount, when the tractor reached the brow of the hill that descended from the farmhouse to the South fields. As the reader can likely anticipate, the increase in speed as we arrived at the downward slope wrong-footed me somewhat, and I soon found myself struggling to match the pace of the tractor. Worse still, my difficulty did not go unnoticed by the other boys who – for the first time, I might add – began to take interest in my pursuit.

Taking the view that I couldn't keep pace for long, I made a bold though confident jump onto the trailer as soon as I had struggled it back within my reach. To my delight, I found sure footing on the plate and a fine grasp on the top of the trailer's tailgate. I was aboard.

My success, rather predictably, signalled the end of the brief interest of all the boys; all, that is, except Hamish. The youngest but me, he had long been my closest rival (the others, I imagine, saw neither of us as threatening enough for competition). Sitting in the corner next to the tailgate, Hamish eyed me with no little hatred. His expression is the last I can remember of the event. The rest was related to me as follows:

Just as I was lifting my first leg up and into the trailer the wheels hit a sizable rock in the track, bouncing the trailer, boys and me abruptly into the air. Obviously when one is sitting safely on the flat-bed the worst that was likely to happen was a hard knock on the backside. Unfortunately, for one in the middle of a heroic ascent, the result was considerably more severe. The bounce, I was told, lifted me some feet from the footplate and disturbed my balance sufficiently to ensure that on the way back down I missed it completely.

For another boy of my age, the game would, perhaps, have ended right there in a abrupt and messy pile on the road. Not so, however for a boy blessed with the swift reactions of the family Brown. Unfortunately for me, those swift reactions were to cost me dear.

It was with a speed of movement that the boys found difficult to properly relate afterwards, that my hands instinctively grabbed hold of the tailgate. As my body weight continued downward, however, that firm hold of safety became the noose around my neck. You see, instead of remaining securely in the upright position, the tailgate came free from it's latch and crashed violently down from the vertical to the horizontal. At this point, dear reader, no man could have avoided disaster.

At some point on my (now uncontrollable) descent, my chin came hard into contact with the fallen trailer door, knocking me – the boys later related – out cold before I disappeared from their sight and onto the road. Scared to reveal to the farmer what had occurred, the boys stayed silent until they reached the South fields, abandoning me to my unconsciousness. Realising I was missing, the farmer soon got the story out of them and, cursing all the while about what he would tell my Father, ran up the hill to recover me.

He found me insensible in the middle of the track. At first I believe he thought I was dead but, fortunately, with the help of water splashed liberally about the face, I came round. I was, however, in something of a poor way. Yes, I was dirty and battered and my chin was much abused, but these were not of primary concern. Rather more worrying, and creating a substantial volume of blood, was a deep gash behind my right ear.

The doctor was sent for immediately. He did not arrive for three hours, by which time the damage was irreparable.

***

Now, though no one was quite sure, the boys thought it likely that while the tailgate was responsible for my chin they were, nonetheless, reasonably sure that it was the footplate that dealt me that second, more severe blow to the ear. Or so went, at least, the story related to the doctor when he finally arrived and began asking questions. Of this I have no memory: I was already in bed, being nursed by Lotti.

The doctor's examination revealed that, in addition to deep cuts to the chin and head, I was reacting to stimuli in an oddly disoriented manner. More worryingly still, he said, was a fierce and persistent ringing in the damaged ear.

Unsure of what else to do (knowledge of head injuries was not as advanced as it is nowadays) the doctor prescribed a full week of bed rest and advised that I was not to exert myself beyond a slow walk for the coming three months.

On a cheerful note, I am happy to report that they were a rather blissful seven days and nights that I spent with Lotti at my side. Indeed, so blissful were they that I was not a little upset when my Father came to collect me when those days of bed-rest were up.

I was taken back to our family home and was not to return to the farm until well into adulthood. While the ringing has dissipated, the hearing in my right ear has never fully returned.

***

I should perhaps explain to the reader why I am reluctant to call the event an 'accident'.

Those of you familiar with the construction of safety latches on the tailgates of farm trailers will know that they are not in the habit of falling simply because of a bump in the road: the latches are designed with exactly that sort of rough treatment in mind and, as a result, do not routinely fail under such everyday rigours.

No, dear reader, it is my belief that Hamish unlatched the tailgate at the moment he saw that my mount was successful. You see, such a self-assured, and *masculine*, display on my part could not but have changed the 'pecking order', as it were, and would certainly have deprived him of what little social advantage he had over me. This he could not have allowed to happen.

Making enquiries to Lotti in the period after the incident, I discovered no evidence to contradict my theory regarding Hamish, though I did discover plenty to support it. Most telling, of course, was Hamish's perverse sense of humour. While the others, (and, yes, even me) eventually allowed ourselves a quiet laugh in the face of the almost-far-worse disaster, Hamish, on the other hand, found the incident *suspiciously* entertaining. In the coming months he was even brazen enough to recount the tale to the other farm hands not once, nor twice, but frequently. Though I was never able to press Lotti for a precise number, I was always given to understand that it was figure significantly higher than she thought proper.

History has been poorly served these past years, dear reader. What occurred that day was no accident. Let me repeat: I, Herman Brown, assert that Hamish deliberately unlatched the trailer; an act of sabotage that resulted in the permanent loss of hearing in my right ear.

That in recent years Hamish (unsuccessfully) proposed marriage to Lotti makes my suspicions doubly justified. Hamish, you see, always resented an historical intimacy between Lotti and me that had occurred in the years before my summer at the farm.

Lotti and I, I should point out, were something of childhood sweethearts in our infancy (or 'kissing cousins' as it is sometimes more colloquially known). And, while completely innocent, our intimacy was something of a family joke. I think it more than likely that Hamish, eavesdropping on a private conversation, became cognisant of this childhood attachment and decided to undermine it.

That he would have recourse to such violent intervention is not only possible but plausible and certainly it was consistent with the local reputation of his family; particularly his father, Sandy Lyon.

It was clear then – and from what little I have heard since, this was only confirmed in adulthood – that Hamish, like his father before him, was an unscrupulous and immoral bastard.

I Dream of Mikhail Gorbachev

(An Extract from Russian Government Files)

Donald S Murray

16 Cairnbost
Isle of Raws

6ᵗʰ October 1999

My Dear Mikhail,

I am writing to you because I am alone and I know you are too. The kids have left home now and Andy's in his usual place, sitting in the corner of the Smithy Bar with a nip and a half-pint in front of him. No doubt he'll be mumbling too about how he'd do anything for his country and how the English are always keeping him and the rest of us Scots down. It's not that I've ever noticed him clambering to his feet to do anything about it. After all, as my father used to say, it's far easier for the likes of Andy to moan about how someone else is glueing his bum to his seat than shoving a thistle down the back of his breeks to get him off it.

 Anyway, I shouldn't complain. You're alone for different, sadder reasons. Your wife, Raisa's gone now, taken from your side by cancer, and today and for the rest of your life, you face the prospect of living your days without her. I feel for you, my dear, sweet Mikhail with your dark eyes touched by sadness, that crimson mark always on your face, when I think of how lonely it must be for you now. There is no doubt she was bright and beautiful, a remarkable woman of her or any other time. I can remember so many things about her – how she made the little children of Reykjavik laugh and smile at all her stories, driving Nancy Reagan mad with jealousy at the way she charmed them all and what she said when she came to London that year – that she would rather visit Marks and Spencer than go to Karl Marx's grave. How you must have chuckled when she came out with things like that. How too she must have made the old comrades around you bristle and choke in fury, muttering about how unsuitable she was for a man in your position, a leader of the Communist Party, the one in charge of the entire Soviet Union. For all their complaints, there is no doubt that someone like that would have lightened your eyes and heart when shadows came to your family later in life. There was the time, for instance, when these nasty, brutish generals, all trying to bring the old ways and certainties back, imprisoned you inside your holiday home. There was the moment too when, for all your smartness and intelligence, you realised that power had been snatched from you by an old, drink-sodden clown.

There is a man in our community whom I know must feel like that. Every time I see his face at the front of the kirk, I think of you, Mikhail. Alasdair has the same sad eyes, balding head, even a red birthmark just like yours though, in his case, it spreads along his right cheek. He wears the same grey hat and coat as you did too, a dark scarf around his neck. I watch him take these off every time he goes to kirk – hanging the coat and scarf in the vestibule, placing his hat on a peg – and I remember the days he used to come to our house when he was younger and turned his eyes shyly in my direction, his mouth becoming dry of words each time he looked at me.

It was my father he spoke to most. He'd talk to him about hiring out his tractor and the money he made hauling peats home for this or that one. He had a digger, too, and he'd sit in it for hours on end, scooping a ditch out of some boggy, waterlogged stretch of land or digging the foundations for a home.

'Steady as he goes, Mr Morrison. Steady as he goes. That's what they always say about me. Steady as he goes.'

'You're Mr Perfection when you sit behind these controls.' Dad would nod and smile. 'You've got a great reputation in this place, Alasdair. There's no denying that.'

'Och, well,' he'd blush, 'It's like my own father always told me. You've got to guard your own name on this island. Make sure you look after it as carefully as you can. There's all too many ready to steal it from you. And once you do, you'll never get it back.'

'Aye. Aye.' Dad would turn away, raising his eyebrows and looking in my direction. There were times he'd pretend to stifle a mock-yawn when Alasdair was in his company. 'Mr Steady and Serious,' he called him behind his back. 'So slow he keeps stalling.'

He wasn't the only one who found him that way. The village girls weren't slow in letting me know how tedious they found my admirer to be.

'He's not here again, is he?' Mairi might ask.

'You fairly draw a good crop of Casanovas to this crofthouse, don't you, Elizabeth? How can you put up with the likes of him?'

Yet I now see he would have been fairly easy to put up with. I watch his hands these days as he puts his Bible before him on the pew. They're strong hands. Neat and clean. Nails trimmed and clipped. Skin scrubbed and unsullied by any of the dirt left behind after his work. There's a wholesome smell about him too. Soap and a tiny splash of after-shave. Imperial Leather. A bottle that must have been bought twenty years ago. Suit pressed. Shirt ironed. Shoes polished. There's not even a speck of dandruff on his shoulders.

And all that cleanliness is not just part of his appearance. It's also in the way he acts and talks and behaves. There is the consideration he displays when a woman enters the kirk alongside him. He opens the door, ushers her through, and all the time, he is speaking softly, graciously, talking that way to everyone he encounters in his daily business.

'Is there anything else you'd like me to do?' he says when he's finished his work. 'Remember to call me anytime you'd like.'

I imagine he's much like you in that way: the quiet, ready smile for others, the way you'd succeed in winning over even those with whom you disagreed, people like Ronald Reagan and Margaret Thatcher. (She even said the first time you met that you were a man with whom the West could do business.) And you know, for once, she was right. Here was a man with whom all mankind could do business. Someone on whom the whole world could build its trust.

I want to confess something to you, Mikhail. I turned down a man who could be relied on and trusted. A Mr Steady As He Goes. A gentleman with a sound reputation. He turned to me one evening after he had finished clearing out one or two of the drains on my father's croft. It was work he never charged for, hoping, perhaps, that his generosity might encourage someone like me to look at his sad, brown eyes with favour. When he had finished working, he sat in the kitchen, swallowing – as neatly and tidily as he always did – the tea and scones I had prepared for him.

'Elizabeth,' he said, 'Can I ask you something?'

'Yes?'

'Would you like on a date with me? Perhaps for a meal, eh? To the Imperial Hotel in town or some place else you might like? Or a dance or a concert sometime? Or even for a wee run somewhere to Marnwick perhaps or Sulishader?'

He may have said more. He had a tendency to ramble sometimes, allowing his words to race and blur together, digging a ditch for himself with his speech. But I barely heard him. Instead, I was picturing the mocking faces of my friends, the embarrassment I would feel if they ever heard of this request. *'What? The tractor-driver? What made him think he could ever reverse his way into your bed? You let him park too long on your sofa.'* I imagined a lifetime of small humiliations and embarrassments. The jokes and jibes they would all make at my expense.

I said no.

'You're sure?' he asked. 'You can take time and think it over.'

'I'm sure.'

They are words I have regretted coming out of my mouth a thousand times since, Mikhail, but all I saw that day before me was a man whose only pillow-talk would consist of a thousand tales about tractors, the size of their loads and engines, the tracks and trails he had successfully taken his giant wheels and trailers that day.

'You know what I did the first time I got that new tractor of mine? Took her right to the top of the beinn just to see what I could do with it, how I could push her to the limit.'

(I've just had a thought, Mikhail. You must be familiar with men like Alasdair. You probably came across quite a few in the time you were Governor of some region or other, making sure there were record harvests to boast about on Radio Moscow in the days they seemed to mention nothing else on that station. You had a grandfather, too, who was sent into exile for failing to grow crops even though he had never been sent any seeds to plant to begin with. And there were also the years you spent as the driver of a combine harvester in the collective farm where your family lived, the time that earned you entrance into university, made sure you took your first steps towards that sparkling career you had.)

Yet to return to Alasdair, I splintered his heart that day, blasted it into tiny fragments with the way I refused to go out with him. And he reacted to all with dignity. A shrug of his shoulders. A sad twist to his lips.

'That's okay, Elizabeth. I had the feeling you might not.'

It was after that I met Andy. Distrusting him a little even that first time we met, he was a man who reacted very differently when I refused his request for a date. 'My dear Madam,' he declared, 'you are turning down the experience of a lifetime. A night in your life – and perhaps even more – you will look back on as one of the most sensational and unforgettable in your experience. Elizabeth, I ask you again, will you come out with me?'

This time I said yes.

Looking back, it is so easy to see why I was fooled. He was so different to Alasdair, a red-faced, dark-haired, untidy man whose feet were rarely rooted to the earth. Instead, they rolled upon the ocean, stepping on the decks of Merchant Navy ships that travelled across the Pacific, Atlantic, the Mediterranean Sea. He'd talk about them from time to time, either by my side or across the kitchen table from my father. '*Murmansk. Vladivostok. The Crimea. I've been to all these places,*' he'd say, '*Poor bloody places. They all were. Poor bloody places.*' And with words like these, he swept me up too, moving across the floor of the local hall, crooning songs into my ear.

'Calamine Lotion. It's good for the skin,' he'd sing, parodying the words of a Gaelic waltz. Or 'Dance. Dance. Dance to the ten guitars.'

Yet I was swayed even more by the words of the other girls. They beamed every time he opened his mouth, laughing at his jokes, marvelling at how far he had travelled.

'He's some man, that Andy,' they might say.

'I wouldn't mind a night or two with him, Liz. If only you hadn't got your mitts on him first.'

'God. You're a lucky, lucky woman.'

Sometimes, though, I'd catch his expression after we'd spent the weekend drinking and dancing with our usual crowd. I'd be aware of a darkness in his eyes, a look of desperation, as if all his wildness was an attempt to escape from himself, to evade the shadows that sometimes threatened to overwhelm him. There was one night he was sick after a party over in Maransay. His head was bowed, stomach retching, as he leaned against a wall.

'God,' he'd say, 'Elizabeth. I hate my Dad. The way he used to treat Mam. Always drinking. Wasting his money. And I'm scared that I might turn out that way. Don't let me, Elizabeth. Don't let me. You can stop me doing that. You're my protection. You're my wall...'

He stumbled then – the wall failing to keep him upright, his feet giving way. As I hauled him up again, he turned towards me, his eyes wet and tearful, mouth slobbering.

'You see too much, Elizabeth. You do. You see too much...'

No. I did not, Mikhail. At least not then. I didn't see the time that was coming for me, for him and us. He thought I'd be the saving of him. It turned out instead to be the wrecking of me, my children David and Michelle who turned their backs on our home as soon as they could. They had no time for the loop of drink and late nights that Andy coiled and fastened around our lives together. They wanted to escape the heat of his sudden rages, the coldness of the grudges – against his father, neighbours, even the English – he nursed within.

You, too, my dear Mikhail, must have suffered a similar blindness to my own. You failed, perhaps, to see the dangers in the white-haired, red faced old man who clambered onto the turret of a tank in Moscow, telling them to turn around their wheels and drive away from the capital, that there could be no return to the bad old days of Brezhnev and Stalin, the old men who stood for hours in their Astrakhan hats on a balcony overlooking Red Square, watching the missiles roll by, troops strut past, the rifles on their shoulders, eyes forward, arms raised in salute.

You must have been grateful to him then. Boris Yeltsin. Saviour of perestroika, glasnost, the democratic experiment you began. Only to watch despairingly as that man betrayed you and others, the Red Flag you had known and loved all your days. Seen him, too, in his sudden, drunken rages. The moments he would stand in front of a band in a foreign capital and, waving a baton in his band, try his best to conduct them. The times when he would lie sprawled within the seat of an Aeroflot liner while a group of waiting politicians tapped their feet restlessly in front of a red carpet stretched out in front of an airport terminal.

I recall moments like these, too, happening in my life with Andy. The night he pretended to play lead guitar along with the Spectrums at a dance in Cairnbost Hall, asking them to play 'Your Cheating Heart' and 'Peigi A'Ghraidh.' The day he failed to turn up for Michelle's wedding, still drunk from the night before. The minister's feet tapping impatiently, clasping the Bible in his hand.

'Well, where is he? When is he going to turn up?'

On days like these I feel the same embarrassment you must have experienced the many times you watched that oaf disgrace the position you had honoured some years before. When I hear him stumbling through the doorway late at night, collapsing down the stairs he was trying his best to climb. Or the nights his hand is on the handle of my bedroom door, hammering away because, terrified of him, I have placed a chair tight against it. Hearing him yell.

'Let me in, woman! Why the hell don't you let me in?'

It's on nights like these, while I lie trembling and afraid, I think of what life might be like with other men. Those like you, Mikhail or Alasdair. Those whom the world misunderstands and sometimes mistreats. Dismissing them as dull and boring. Condemning them for how right-minded and respectable they are, their decency and sense of duty, how the way they are so serious and considerate and kind seems to suck the very heart and soul out of them. And I blame all the rest of us for being far too aware of the tiny flaws and faults the world sees in such men. The red stains that blotch and mark their skin. The way they can be tedious and boring at times. The long dull conversations that might be found on the lips of those men who drive the likes of combine harvesters, diggers, tractors...

It's on nights like these, too, I dream of the likes of Mikhail Gorbachev and long to have chosen their kind to lie by my side. It's on nights like these I dream.

With all my love at your time of loss and need,

Elizabeth

The Greatest Magician I Ever Knew

Lynsey May

Now I don't want you to think I'm the kind to go spilling secrets. Not really the done thing in this line of work, but there does come a certain point in the evening, that post show witching hour, right about now actually, when a nice cold drink does tend to loosen the tongue. Here's the deal, you promise to hit the bar in the next five minutes and I'll teach you a card trick or two. Not good enough? Well then, get me a double and I might just tell you about the greatest magician I ever knew.

Now talking about Eric, it's thirsty work, so don't be stingy with the shots and before we start, it's best you know that there's those folk who're drawn to magic for its subtle skills and intricacies – and those who simply love to lie. Don't you be sitting there judging, not 'til you've felt the thrill of fooling a room of people who think they can't be fooled. There's nothing better, not even sex.

But magic, it's as fickle as any bedfellow I've had. It's not all applause and beautiful, baffled faces in the audience and there's been plenty of nights I've crawled home burning with shame, fingers still fidgeting from a fluffed trick. But you don't even have to screw it up to be a failure these days.

Do you know how many shows there are in the Fringe? Do you know how many promoters and performers crawl away from Edinburgh with their tails between their legs and their pockets scraped empty once August ends? Have you tried competing with a fucking iPhone? Half the folks that do pay for tickets sit there, tinkering away, square eyed and immune to wonder. It's enough to make a girl cry. That's the thing though, isn't it, you need to have a thick skin when it comes to magic – and young Eric, well.

We met three years into my career at a shady little venue in Edinburgh's old town, back when I was just starting to make a name for myself and there were folks still saying I'd go far. Not at that gig though. It was a battle of the bands style affair put on for the Festival – five minutes to show your shit and an audience vote to get through to the next stage, not my cup of tea at all.

I never even watched poor Eric's set, so pissed off was I with my 'wham, bam, no thank you ma'am' reception. But we ran into each other slinking out the back door, and what can I say? History was made. We repaired to the pub and that shy boy and I spent many hours putting the world of magic to rights. And then, well, we did what any two young people would do on a cold night filled with disappointment.

Of course, we put off showing each other our wares until we'd had a good few nights of shagging. It's a vulnerable thing, trying to trick someone who knows what you're doing, and I was right to be reticent because that boy had the slickest hands and most graceful manipulations I'd ever seen. Once the show and tell was over, we were right back to bed.

Partnering up was only natural and I'll admit it, he seemed a shy and bumbling thing then, but I knew, like so many of us woman do, that with a little bit of guidance, he'd end up a great man. And I thought it was worth it didn't I, because over our many long hours putting a show together, hitching from city to city, gig to gig, I learned the secret behind his astounding sleight of hand. Little Eric, only three years old, contracted an unusual disease that kept him confined to a hospital bed for 11 long, lonely years. What better way to amuse yourself than learning how to make the nurse's dreaded syringe disappear before her very eyes? The wee lamb. And there it was. I was already hooked, but that story had me lined-and-sinkered too.

To my mind, those hospital shows were the root of his shyness and I worked out ways to disguise it and showcase his slickness instead. Because you and me both know, it's not just what your hands are doing, its what you're eyes are saying, what your throat is crooning – that's where the money is.

A few months with me and his shyness was a thing of the past and our show was drawing crowds like you wouldn't believe. We weren't just local any more. We were doing the rounds, London, Berlin. There was even talk of New York. No matter that I was relegated to sidekick, this was what dreams are made of. Not that it lasted, no trick lasts forever.

After a year or two at the top, he became known as a magician's magician — as skilled as they come, but old fashioned with outdated card tricks and a passé smiley assistant. We could both see the way the world was turning, people didn't want deft hands and quiet magic, they wanted bloody levitating, sword wielding superheroes. We had a slot at Euro Disney, that pushed him over the edge. Drunk afterwards, he howled over the lost art and I knew then it was the beginning of our sorry end.

I still say though, Eric was the greatest magician I ever knew. It's not just the skills he perfected or the tricks he wrote himself, it was something much tougher to share. And I'm only sharing it now because the Eric I knew is no more. Don't get me wrong, he didn't crawl back to his hotel room and garrotte himself with a string of silk ties, although there were times I thought that was where we were heading.

No, all those years I was convinced Eric's problem was that he didn't know how to lie, they were the years I was in the dark. Eric is no more because Eric never was.

The bloke's name was Richard when he met me outside that scabby Edinburgh theatre and it's Steven Sword now. You might have seen him on telly. If not, you can look him up online later – who am I kidding, Google him on your phone right now, why don't you? I'll not blame you. His story's always going to be better than mine, because it turns out, the little bastard never was in hospital, never was a shy young man, never was someone needing love and care and compassion to bring him out his shell. He never was any of those things. He was a magician just starting out who needed a sexy assistant and a helping hand getting a foot in the door. Clever him, found a fool to give him her good name and do it for free.

Steven Sword might be drawing the crowds in New York, and you folks with your Googling, you'll have found plenty of claims he's the best in the business, but I'm here to tell you it's not Steven with his flashy tricks that's the greatest. It's Eric who disappeared my knickers and my prospects in the blink of an eye. It's Eric who showed me how an illusion can become a life. And it's Eric who will always be the greatest magician I ever had the misfortune to know.

Love poem from heart to belly

Katherine McMahon

You are so round! You are the softest
shape, you holder of senses. Did you know
that you have more neurons than a cat's brain?
You don't need to be so down on yourself,
you're a smart cookie, a clever sausage,
the tastiest pie in the oven.
Your stretch marks? I think they look like currents
in the sea on a calm day. Currents are essential
to the ecosystem, did you know that?
David Attenborough explained it to me –
it's all about the micro-organisms. You stir up
feelings like plankton
for me to feast on, my whale mouth eager,
turning them into strong muscles, into leaps
and tail fins. Scientists are always speculating
about whales' breaches, did you know that?
Like joy isn't a good enough explanation.
It's good enough for me.
You make me sing.

Skin Care

Leyla Josephine

There was a woman
She was thirty two years old
and looked seventeen.

She smiled sympathetically when I told my age
twenty three
she had guessed
thirty.

I recently found three, burrowed, lines
under each eye
indicating,
my body, despite my efforts,
is in fact,
getting older.

I asked her what her secret was
how her skin looked so smooth
so fresh,
so unused, so unlike mine.

She talked me through ten steps she performs every morning, every night.
Her skin routine.

The Eye Makeup Removal
The Cleanse
The Exfoliator
The Refresher
The Booster
The Essence
The Ampoule
The Sheet Mask
The Eye Cream
and finally
The Moisturizer

How can she be fucked? ten minutes every morning, ten minutes every night
that's twenty minutes a day washing her face?

Oh
and never sleep with your make up on
and always wear at least factor fifty.

She walked away and I was still in shock.
I wear my make up to bed more often than not.
I usually stay up late, stealing as many minutes from the day as I can.
I rarely think ahead,
I definitely don't have a face wash plan.

I've worked out that this woman spends two hours thirty three minutes a week
washing her face.

Thats's one hundred and twenty one hours every three hundred and sixty five days,
which is five days a year.

If this woman lives till she's seventy two,
she will have spent a whole year of her life washing her fucking face.

It sounds like some sort of Cat Deeley torture camp
sponsored by Instagram
and it's definitely not for me.

Think of all the things she could do with that extra year
backpacking in nepal, learning to play the piano,
pilot lessons, scuba diving, she could have had a baby, or cycled across
a country. or maybe she could have just chilled the fuck out.

So towards the end of my journey if anybody asks me why I look so old
I'm going to tell them that I have lived every minute I could not washing my face.

When my grandchildren ask me what age I am,
I'll tell them i've laughed one million more times than my age and have had more
friends than the age spots on my hands
and I'm fifty times as old as how many times I've fucked their grandfather,
now fuck off.

I'll tell them about all the adventures I've been on, how much trouble I've been in.

I'll tell them to stay up as late as they can and sleep in as long as they want

And to go on holiday
and wear minimum sun screen because everyone looks better with a tan.

And I'll show them my scars and tell them all about the arguments that I won and lost
and I'll tell them if they want to pick at scabs then they should
because skin heals and it moulds to your story
and you'll never know anything if your always careful and you'll never learn any
lessons if you stay safe and that behaving is
boring.

I'll tell them late nights staying up drinking is a privilege denied to many
traveling is a privilege denied to many,
I'll tell them that growing old is a privilege denied to many.

so don't give a fuck about gray hair
it shows that you cared about something
the flabbing belly is a testimony to your children
your dangling boobies look fab
and who doesn't like things that wibble or wobble.

The bags under your eyes are evidence of the deep conversations that went into the
night
your sagging bingo wings are proof that you carried
your soft skin shows that you were tender
just stay healthy,
but smoke if you enjoy it, drink if you enjoy it,
dance all the time but especially with friends,
try not to forget.
Don't hate yourself because, trust me, there are enough people in life that will do
that for you

and for fuck sake do not spend 20 minutes a day washing your face.

Beer Belly

Patricia Ace

On the common by the Underground
trees uprooted by October's catastrophe
bear toddlers in their branches. Mothers,
braced by pushchairs, stand, fixed in time and space.

From the squats wafts dub-style reggae,
the harshsweet reek of sticky buds.
The trust-fund hippies light a bonfire,
trailing whippets tied to strings.

I'm wearing vintage Biba from Dot's stall
at Deptford market; my grant blown again
on dungarees, dropped waists and Empire lines.
He said his Dad would send a cheque

but some beds were made to lie in.
I've put my parents visit off till later in the year.
Meanwhile I'm buying one size up
and blaming it on beer.

Upon Eating a Milky Way Crispy Roll

Judith Kahl

Delicate business, this,
trying to strip chocolate off wafer
without melting it.
Then, even more precarious:
breaking and lifting the wafer
off the White Soft Stuff, which
reminds me –

That time when my cousin and I
collected snails behind her family's shed in the rain,
young enough to be free
of fear or disgust;
able see beauty in spirals
and slow moist bodies.
She won this game (again)
by plucking a pale white and yellow creature
off a leaf.
It was the queen of snails.
(For beauty necessitated femininity.)
So enchanted, so bewitched were we
that we began to undress her
with trembling fingers
and serious faces
which slowly
turned
into
bewilderment
then shock and panic,
at the sight of twitching tubes
which helplessly bathed in slime,
grimy innards mingled with children's tears,
sticky fingers wiped on slippery leaves and
she ran first and I –

Yeah I don't really want this anymore.

Catching my eye

Hazel Buchan Cameron

How do I explain to the farmer
whose wall I've just crashed through
that it was his lamb with the pure
black face that caught my eye,
as I thought of a friend about to die.

Sitting amongst the accident debris,
I watch the lamb leap under its mother.
Then – through the rear view mirror
a rainbow stretches across the valley.
I recall that if viewed from on high
it can make a complete, glorious eye.

The Six-Foot

Callum McSorley

I think the reason I find it hard to write this down is because I'm mostly ignorant and dumb and the more I think about things the more I realise I don't know anything. I'm not sure it matters much anyway but here it is:

In the summer of 2015 I was working on the railways, mostly on the West Coast Mainline, refurbishing footbridges. I stripped off the flaky paint and rust with a flap-disc grinder and needle gun, cleaned it with standard thinners and recoated it in thick alloy primer that stuck to my skin. I scratched and peeled it off in the shower afterward, leaving my arms pink and new.

We built scaffold on the tracks to reach the outside and underneath of the parapet, so the work was all night shift. Fifty hours per week. This maybe had something to do with my complete and utter breakdown, but that also could have started back when I graduated uni, then spent the next two years hosing shit off car tyres. Or it was maybe when I was thirteen and hit my sister hard and felt so guilty I thought I should just kill myself. My father died when I was four but I don't think events are so far reaching. Or at least I hope not.

The squad consisted of seven guys, most of them older than me with years of experience of painting and labouring and a hatred of their wives that I could never tell if it was put on or not. When I got home at six in the morning I would hold Lisa tight and sob when she left me for work. Did they do the same or were they really so happy to be away from their families for fifty hours a week, and longer if you count having to sleep all day?

'She says to me: "your heart's a swingin brick," our supervisor would often say. Or, 'I could've kicked her cunt in before I came out the night.' He was always kind to me, and was a socialist through and through. He campaigned for worker's rights and against knife crime and knew Tommy Sheridan to talk to.

The point of rubbing the metal with thinners after grinding off the top layer of paint is that it takes off the film of dust left behind and evaporates much more rapidly than water. This fine dust was potentially very dangerous if breathed in. We were never sure if the paint was lead-based or not so we always wore paper suits that were supposed to be burned afterwards and full-face respirators that buzzed like Darth Vader when you breathed and cut off your peripheral vision. The visor would steam up if the mask wasn't face-fit so you would know you were filling your lungs with shit. Blood tests were irregular. Lead poisoning makes you go mad before it kills you.

You can only go on the tracks once you're granted possession of the line and isolation if there is Overhead Line Equipment. We spent a lot of time talking and smoking. I didn't talk much but laughed a lot.

'When I was seventeen I had a revelation,' the super said. 'I was just walking down the street and suddenly thought, "hang on a minute, Michael Jackson isnae a hard man!" Think about it: Beat It, Bad, Smooth Criminal. His songs are about being hard, but he isnae. The boys are lookin for a scrap and the man starts gein it laldy on the dance floor.'

I'm a small man. My head is small and my face too. Too small to fit the mask and ear defenders and hard hat all at once. The hat would balance on top of my head and regularly fell off, leaving me swearing and punching the deck as it bounced off the side of the scaffold and plunged six meters down to the track.

Three lifts up, the top of the scaffold, I would cautiously step over the OLE, lifting my steelies high like a diver walking on the bottom of the ocean, regarding it as some dangerous wild animal, only resting. A viper. Earths were put up at either side of the worksite as a failsafe. The first time my foot clipped it I almost tripped. I dropped to my knees and hugged the handrail. 280,000 volts when live. It would melt you before your heart stopped. Then it would kill everyone on or near the bridge if it arced.

The manager, the guy above the super, was young for his position. He didn't know yet if he was David Brent or Gordon Ramsey. The popular consensus was that he was an incompetent prick and his girlfriend was shagging everything she could get her hands on behind his back. 'The filth is pourin out of her,' the super said, looking at her Facebook profile. 'Reekin of it. I can just tell.' He claimed he could tell in a split second what somebody was all about. At the training course to get our Personal Track Safety ticket he took one look at the teacher and declared: 'He's a ravin alcy.'

They taught us the names for each part of the track. The ditch on each side of a pair of running lines is called the cess. The distance of the sleeper between the rails is the four-foot. The gap between a set of up and down lines is the six-foot. These aren't the actual distances, just the terms used. If you're on the track and a train is coming in both directions the safest thing to do is lie down in the six-foot. If you stand you could be pulled into the train by the slipstream.

The manager, whose girlfriend was busy being fucked at home while we were out hammering rust from the stair treads in Anniesland, was also in charge of site safety: the COSS. It was the popular consensus he would get someone killed one day. I never really spoke to him, just nodded and grunted. He would pick his girlfriend up from nights out on his way home from a shift and she would sit on the couch full of it while he tried to sleep upstairs. I felt sorry for him because everyone thought he was an arsehole, but then he'd always open his mouth and my sympathy would vanish like so much paint thinner.

'The reason the firms died out in the 90's was all the ecstasy,' the super said. 'You'd bump into a guy at the dancing who you'd been wantin to walk up and down with yer steelies on and instead of fightin you'd have your arm round him, best of pals, makin plans for the morrow, "We've gotta do that! Give us a phone!"'

I worked nights for months, the time passed slowly but at the same time seemed to just disappear behind me as night became day then night again and I was back at work feeling on the brink of panic. This is probably normal, I thought.

In words, it seems much more trivial than it felt at the time. Or maybe I can't remember it well enough to tell it properly. Pain is quickly forgotten, it's a survival mechanism, a product of evolution to keep us living and reproducing.

One night I hit my head off the handrail as I bent down to pick up my brush. Wearing a hard hat the sensation is painless but the noise amplified. My hat bounced off the tower onto the ballast below. It's a white hat, those new to the railway wear blue ones.

I climbed down, latex gloves getting wet and cold from the aluminium ladders. At the bottom I picked up my hat and switched the headlamp back on. I looked out through the dark across the railway bridge. In the distance I could see the marker board blinking red on the other side of the bridge. It signifies the limit of the worksite. If a train has to stop at the boards because of a timing error the company responsible are charged five thousand pounds a minute until it gets on its way. I took off my ear defenders and let the painful din of the gennies and needle guns rattle my teeth. Then I walked out towards the blinking light. Ballast to ballast, so you don't slip on a wet concrete sleeper. I concentrated on my feet, the steel plates showing through the holes in the toes of my safety boots. Going across the bridge I saw graffiti on the inside of the parapet. Somebody else had come along here without safety boots or a hard hat or orange high vis. At the other side of the board I lay down in the six foot, imagining two trains were coming towards me in both directions. My headlamp shone up into a clear sky. The OLE bisected the moon. I switched the lamp off. I thought about Lisa and my dad and my friends and family, big thoughts about my life which at the time were imbued with some great romantic meaning but which now I think about it seem small and silly, rambling and disconnected. Fragments as far apart as one star to the next. The dew point was setting in and I shivered in my overalls and paper suit. I got scared and double-timed it back to Anniesland station and the footbridge.

If you need to stop a train you place three detonators on the track twenty metres apart then stand 100 metres ahead of the last detonator and wave a torch vigorously from a point of safety.

The manager, the COSS, was busy putting stair treads in and hadn't missed me. The super was smoking and telling a story about the time he broke into someone's house with a baseball bat on Hallowe'en while dressed as Jermaine Jackson. It turned out to be the wrong house and he scared the shit out of an old couple who were sitting watching the telly. Bat behind his back he apologised and left. The police later caught up with him and the rest of the Jackson Five, all blacked up, they asked his name and he replied: 'I'm Jermaine, this is Tito...'

I quit then. None of the squad got in touch while I was in the hospital or after I left. I miss my supervisor. I stayed indoors for a good while and slept at night next to Lisa. At some point it will be time to go back to work.

How Slowly Glue Dries

Collette Rayner

Hobby

Worlds

For the purpose of this enquiry, *'Hobby'* is the meta-narrative and comes before the sub-narrative of insular worlds.

The Model Rail Enthusiast | The Drone Hobbyist | The Micro-Nationalist

The above three hobbyist organisations appear as characters, through which a period of research, interview and conversation is represented and relayed.

To the left is the *model rail male*, in the middle sits the *drone man* and to the right of him is the *micro-nationalist*.

The operation of each organisation relies on its own insular communities to promote an environment in which the sharing of knowledge and tools amongst their members/fellow enthusiasts/citizens is paramount.

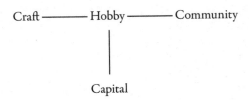

There is nothing that my infatuated mind would desire to see more than the union between these hobbies. However the generative source of these texts could be referred to as 'brief interviews with difficult men'.

Community

The *model rail male* reunites bi-weekly with the clubhouse. In preparation for immersion he recalls how in youth he abstained and now he devours, feasting on the history of locomotives past.

His community lies on a bedrock of anorak and devotion. Well-studied in patient explanation, his version of the miniature divides the width of the spare room, as his newly borrowed tools circumnavigate what was supposed to reside neatly within spare time.

Their most pressing group challenge is the group itself. As numbers fall strategies must be adopted to continue the club and draw younger members in. The discussion of rebranding not only offends the models themselves but also the tools and clubhouse mortar, generating an unspoken schism towards those of 'the prototype generation' (also acknowledged as those whom they will need).

The *drone man* is back in his hack home sharing his knowledge and tools. There are two kind of burning smells that can interrupt conversations here: burning for research (good) and the burning of creative rights (bad, and always government initiated).

As WikiLeaks had so thoughtfully informed him on numerous occasions, the Trans-Pacific partnership was coming soon.

His unmanned vehicles had once needed a man to dedicate all of his out-of- office hours to them: a prolonged ode to sci-fi. Drones: a distilled love song for the hobbyist. Politics is full of hobbyists. Did you know that?

The Trans-Pacific partnership with its Geofencing demands had called out to the drone man: *'Little man. Silly man. This is not your hobby, this is our gunship warship'.* This was creatively bruising, the drone man was quite sure of that.

Annulling his longstanding something with this monocultural society, he turned to his left to acknowledge the *micro-nationalist.* He attempts to bridge their distance with the topic of a permissive *'do-ocracy'.*

Keen to respond with a personal intensity and emphasise his un-renewed membership to the hack house the *micro-nationalist* scoffs: *'Welcome to the hack home: Tool, fetish and small dystopia'*

The statement would have been received differently had the drone man not known it stemmed from insecurity.

The micro-nationalist community was particularly brittle, especially in regards to informal conversation. Their community existed predominantly in the virtual, which led to a lack of club houses, with most interactions conducted online. As a result, gatherings are attended by Disneyfied ideals of what each person believed a sovereign figure should look like. This often undermines the intention of the nation in the first place and simply encourages the typical cinema stereotype of a micro-nation as a comedic entity.

Their biggest concern is to be taken seriously by other nations.

The *micro-nationalist* had attempted on many occasions to reach out to others, as he learned more about his hobby he rooted himself in title, domain name and diplomatic letter headings.

Whilst encouraging of contemporaries he often found himself annoyed by a lack of recognition and response to his correspondence.

That is their way of doing things and this was his. His patience would be acknowledged in some small way, as he knew it should be.

Having sculpted his own national designs on a set of aspirational models, he was dedicated to engaging only with states on the same level of seriousness as him.

The efforts of these hobbyists should not be undersold as the products of ego. All hobbyists will acknowledge that they are all eccentrics but also they are not. They are just a more intense type of people with better ability to recall jargon or relative matter without prompt or hesitation.

Craft

The information immediately rushes forth as if the conversation had already started.

> The craft has entered me: I am altered
> The model has moved me: I am altered
> The knowledge has transported me: I am altered

The *model rail male* is even less enthused by the term hobby than he is by this prototypal generation. Abruptly he divulges: *'I am not a hobbyist, I am an impressionist! I would like to impart on the people, an impression of real transport in miniature.'*

This hobby stems from something more. It is a repeat prescription in something that borders preservation and a wanton story telling.

Model rail is the emulsion in which he coats his fingers and collects all of the other debris from his father's youth. This is the original craft, when the poetics of precision had never known of the poetics of the glitch.

His is the act, which proclaims nothing yet holds its own profundity. That was enough in his mind to be taken seriously in the cathedral of craft.

The *drone man* mouthed despairingly to his right, *'All these toys around but no free time to play.'*

Staring straight ahead, the *rail male* asserts *'not toys, models'*.

The struggle to express his enthusiasm as an artist is equalled only by his own struggle to replicate the exact. Whilst he will admit there can be something sinister in the miniature, there is also a concise revelation.

Unlike him, the *drone man* revels in his hobbyist title.

Worn with the pride of a scouts badge it identifies him as a part-timer and classifies his intentions as harmless. The undertones of his sector are darker and his knowledge goes far deeper, orbiting expert but his intentions are warmer.

The micro-nationalist, avid in his almost constant blogging efforts, has taken to sealing the fissures in his fingertips with superglue.

Not only will this assert that his online efforts are a craft but it may also paint him as a martyr to the cause.

The *micro-nationalist* was confused himself by the term hobbyist. He even felt unsure of whether he should take himself seriously or not.
He represented his nation at all times. Nation, not website, and if he was going to play the game he had to play it right. His purpose whether serious or not was to hone his country. Behaving as if it were real would not only gain him respect from his peers but greater standing in the micro-national world.

His artistry, whilst self righteous, was in his opinion, more revolutionary than drones or train sets.

He did not want to carve out a fight but there was truth in the fact that whenever one scratches the surface, all hobbies stem back to a genuine enquiry.

Besides if society wanted him to speak warmly about unity, it should have behaved better.

Capital

A Logic:'

Breathing in deeply, the *model rail male* stays close to the thing that separates him from paid labour. Free time itself is the western answer to the question hobby.

He began to model as a child, abandoning it in teenage years when hormones informed him that reality has tits and craft is better as beer.

Lying dormant in his spinal column for many years, the modelling never really left.

The repercussions led to an entirely separate career path within the local constabulary. Whilst he made a little pocket money on commissions amongst some members at the clubhouse, a large sum of his salary was as dedicated to the models as he was.

Hobbies are like hurricanes: passions are opposed to reason.

They make us their victims and sweep us away. We feel they must be regulated to weekends and bank holidays, until, released in retirement, passion reigns triumphant.

Unlike the *model rail male*, the *drone man* and *micro-nationalist* were unified in their ability to work remotely.

Having a digital heavy hobby has never attracted as much stigma in youth and has allowed them to intertwine their pastime and profession. Having never repressed their craft, they have little demand to explain their transfer of specialist knowledge.

The *drone man* was very aware that his intelligence was often desired more by the voluntary. With the popularity of drones increasing, he has found occasional employment in achieving sweeping altitude footage for various televised endeavours. This was easy money and encouraging to the ego.

Being a citizen of the United Kingdom, he found himself stalled from folding his career as a programmer too far into his hobby.

It had almost happened with audio digital converters and now it was happening with copyright and patent.

He screeched, *'Hacking and developing are normal hobbyist things, you can't ban technology!'*

If only he could marry the western world to the blissful hobbyist utopia of Chinese piracy, nothing could stop his club: a micro-processing dream where hobbyists are king and creative development reigns supreme. Its potential outdoes the complications of its history.

'You are not allowed in my hobby, you must stay in your own world' interrupts the *micro-nationalist.*

He would not have a hypothetical nation with an ancestry that is hours old outdo his years of hypothetical effort.

He had not slept well for months, the ideas, which have taken hold of him, would not let him rest. He would like to be a hero for his generation and produce more than a website for his efforts.

Administration solidified his ambitions and he was already worth his weight in Bit- coins. In terms of GDP he was one of the wealthiest nations on the planet, with his Internet business + overtime able to support the entire country financially. Holding a world of profundity and always defiant in opposition, he noticed the glue had dried.

Glasgow Fair: Some Victorian Fragments

John Burnett

Glasgow Fair was a jumble of entertainment and raw spirits at the west end of Glasgow Green. To visit it was a stirring experience. It was a whirlpool for the senses – tobacco smoke, sweat, salt herring and sugary sweets, surprising images on the showmen's booths, caged lions and a live, half-tamed crowd. Emotions were distilled down, with actors murdering one another and discovering long-lost sisters as a matter of routine, man-eating beasts threatening, ballad singers retailing the tragic past, as the rituals of courtship moved towards their various ends.

Then it changed. Between the 1850s and the 1960s, the central activity at the Fair was the trip 'doon the watter,' down the River Clyde from the centre of the city, or by train to the coast, and then by steamer through the islands scattered on the edge of the Highlands.

'The Glasgow Fair holidays? What are they?' 'The period in the month of July every year when there is generally most rain, and when consequently all the public works, etc., shut for holidays.' The 'public works' were the shipyards and engineering works for which Glasgow was known to the world. They made a few capitalists rich, and they enabled thousands of managers, professional men and skilled workers to achieve a comfortable living. But they depended on hundreds of thousands of labourers in the engineering shops, factories and quaysides whose muscles made the city function. They carried, cleaned, stirred, poured, signalled and waited; they were cursed and badly paid. In a separate cosmos, up a tenement stair, wives cleaned and mended, fighting sweat, soot and wear, and boiled and fried to produce meals.

The Fair mattered to Glasgow people as much as anything. Before it men cut down on smoking and drinking. 'In the Clyde shipyards piece-workers never work more strenuously... for every hundred rivets hammered home and every plate fitted means a correspondingly better time at the coast for the black squad and their families.' Boys asked one another 'Hoo much hae ye skerd [saved] up for the fair?' And when the Fair arrived, folk lay long in bed, breakfasted on ham and eggs, dressed up and went as a family on day excursions – 'their finery may be imitation, but their pleasure is real.'

The Broomielaw was the cobbled wharf along the north bank of the River from which the steamboats, and many other vessels, departed. It was the meeting place of the sea and the city, facing a line of ships' chandlers, provision merchants, and bars for the sailors. The stone quays, fronted with baulks of timber, faced a salty culvert.

The boats were moored two and three deep, sometimes more, and cargo and livestock were handled among the passenger steamers. Ships were re-arranged over and over so each one in turn had access to the quay, and travellers might have to cross a couple of other boats to reach the one they sought. When a Rothesay carter drowned, he fell in the water while trying to reach the *Vulcan*, '5th off' at Quay 11.

The river was a turbid sewer. Despite Glasgow's investment in a water supply from the Trossachs, it did not introduce sewage purification until 1894. Raw household and industrial effluent such as waste dyestuffs and mordants swilled together. From the city to Renfrew, the river was polluted with fermenting sewage, 'the smooth surface presents the appearance of heavy raindrops falling into it... this is not descending rain, but escaping gas.' The foul smell of the river was said to encourage women to swig whisky from black bottles (which hid the content, which might have been medicinal), from Govan to Greenock.

A steamboat soon left the city. On the banks of the Clyde were fields where livestock grazed and corn ripened, and in July passengers could see hay being harvested ten minutes after they had left the Broomielaw. They passed a few thatched cottages and villages, and the antique burgh of Renfrew at the mouth of the River Cart. For an hour the journey was unremarkable, apart from the always-heavy traffic on the water, boat following (or fouling) small boat. Then the steamer took right and left bends at Dalmuir, and there was the open expanse of the Firth, the steam and smoke of Port Glasgow and Greenock. And there, distant and bumpy, were the Highlands.

The Firth of Clyde is a huge drowned valley, with long narrow lochs and a scatter of individual islands, offering scenery that changes from hour to hour as a ship moves through it. Walking on its shores or sailing through its lochs enabled city folk to engage with the slender arms of the sea, the islands and the hills, with a closeness, a feeling of intimacy, a sense of ownership. It was different from the ooze of the Mersey, or the estuary of the Thames, where Cockneys holidayed on whelks, gin and mudflats.

At Greenock, Gourock and Wemyss Bay were glass-roofed railway stations like conservatories at mansion houses. Then the pier, and all at once the salt tang, sea tangle, ships' shapes, a wake curving through the waves. On the steamer there was much to experience. For the nose, the smell of the tar caulking melting in the heat, the children's oranges, the rich sulphurous aroma of burning coal. For the palate, whisky, lager beer (as it was called), roast beef and boiled potatoes. For the ear, the rhythm of the machinery and the squalling of gulls and weans, the fiddler's music, and the complaints of the loudmouth who had to be heard. It all changed as the sun went round, the whisky made the men less predictable, and the steamer called at another pier.

Dunting into the briny. At one moment, at speed on the water, and tied to a stone jetty, watching the hyperactivity of loading and unloading. The wide-horned shaggy Highland cattle ruminating, the sparkling reflections of the sun on shimmering waves, the water dripping from the tautening cable, a row of buoys with a cormorant standing on each one, and ships circling like raptors as they waited for a strike at the pier.

The travellers could scent the ocean, and see the biggest ships of the day laden with foreign cargoes, some sweet-smelling, others for smelting.

Each Clyde steamer was a set of techniques and travellers which interacted with one another, making a myriad of points of human interest, a handful of which were caught in print. There might be a delay because the deck was being washed after coaling, or a horse being loaded. Once the *Isle of Bute* couldn't steer leaving Rothesay pier because a woman's dress was entangled with the rudder chain. And tales were told of remarkable wit, like the one about a drunk advancing up Rothesay pier when a steamer was about to cast off. 'Wait, A'm comin' too,' he cried. But the gangway had been hauled in. 'A'm gaun tae hell!' Purser: 'Red-funnelled boat – over there!' and the steamer swept out.

One source of magic was the poems and novels of Sir Walter Scott, which were intensely popular and available in cheap editions. The novels *Waverley* (1814, steamboat of the same name 1828) and *Rob Roy* (book and boat both 1818) were about people from the Lowlands or England discovering Highland Scotland and its distinct culture, and the tourist stepping off at Rothesay was doing the same thing. The awareness of ancient Rome brought *Venus*, *Vesta* (a match for her competitors), *Cupid*, *Apollo*, and *Mars*. The wonder is that no one called a Clyde steamer *Euphoria*, but the thought passes, and a salt-caked coaster comes round the Cloch.

Aglaia, the first iron-hulled passenger steamer in the world, was named from one of the Three Graces, who was married the smith Hephaestus, who had his forge on Mount Olympus. 'The Isles of Greece!' had exclaimed a Scots poet of another archipelago where seafarers threaded an engaging labyrinth.

In 1864, a man aged about twenty travelled alone on the *Chancellor* to Arrochar. He wore a lilac striped regatta [light twill] flannel shirt, while plaining drawers, patched, grey tweed trousers with a purple thread running through the cloth, elastic braces, 'priest-grey vest [waistcoat] and coat', and long grey stockings with white tops. He swam and drowned. His clothes were listed in a newspaper so someone would say his name.

The poor, crowded into slums from Cranhill to Crownpoint, were crammed together in rooms at the Coast, or slept in the woods or the cemetery. Residents with gardens paid watchers to repel drowsy Glaswegians. One couple found lodgings for the night, and took for an evening stroll. They returned to find two families sleeping in their room. Landlady: 'Ye took the bed, but no the flair.'

The Clyde Coast was the Coast, not the seaside, and the visitors were coasters. They coasted. 'The trouble with the Coast, is the cost.'

The small shows which had once come to Glasgow for the Fair were strewn around the Firth. There were nut barrows, sweetie stands, wild beast shows and shooting galleries: the proprietor of one at Gourock assured his customers that their shots were landing in Kilcreggan, two miles away across the sea. Another showman exhibited cork models of cathedrals, and while he declaimed he worked with his knife. His material was old bottle-corks, and he had ample supply.

Glasgow was growing at the end of the century, engulfing nearby burghs. It launched heavier ships. The Fair holidays lengthened, and more people travelled. Newspapers talked of records and quoted exaggerated numbers, until one journalist laughed and said that half a million mutton pies had been sold in Rothesay in one weekend. 'How do you get more people into a Rothesay pub at the Fair?' 'Take the wallpaper off the walls.'

Young men elbowed their way through the latest catchphrases – 'Doon the Gallowgate, boys' – 'A'll hae your hat' – 'That's the sort o man I is.' – drinking with full-throated ease.

'I suppose you made a good many pleasant acquaintances during your stay in Rothesay...?' 'Well no; but I met a lot of old friends whom I had never had the good fortune to become acquainted with before.'

At a Rothesay boarding house two young people spot one another. On the first day they cannot speak because they have not been introduced... she drops a glove... they stroll... evening cruise... She is alone because her parents are in the Mediterranean, he because his are in Switzerland. In Glasgow the following week a housemaid buying kippers recognises the fishmonger's son, and the romance is over. The maid and the shop boy have become aspirational.

But all too soon 'twill be ended –
The City will call us again;
I hear the ring of the hammers,
I see the grimy men,
The dust and the dreary routine
Again are coming near,
And it's goodbye to old Rothesay
For another weary year.

The Fair has gone. It left on a flight to the Costa del Sol. Fragments remain: here and there we can find a collapsing jetty transformed from rectangular structure, through the elaborate geometry of decay, to an end in wrack and ruin. The Clyde is no longer crowded with ships, and at the maritime crossroads of the Tail of the Bank the sugar ship *Captayannis* has been lying on its side since 1974, an unresolved problem in marine insurance, an insoluble lump of rusting steel. And the Firth is still there, with fields running down to the shore and woods and moors above; and the water, and the light playing on the water; another ripple, another sunrise, another summer.

Spaso

Grace Cleary

Look at me? Ah'm a right sight. Aw ma pals it the day centre look like me. Alison n Stella n Maxine. We are aw fat? How come? We ur awe lassies bit we aw wear tracky boattums thit are up oor legs, in big, big trainers, like clown shoes? How come? Did ma Mammy talk tae Maxine's Mammy. Did they go tae the same shop tae git the troosers? Is it a uniform? Like school? The school acroass the road hid ties. A wahnteed a tie, bit ma mammy said 'You don't need a tie. You ur it a spechul school. You hivnae got a uniform. How come? Is oor trackies n trainers a 'dafties' uniform? Is that so everybody wull know we ur 'dafties?'

Maxine says naebiddy is apposed tae caw us 'dafties' any mair. They'll go tae jail How come? It's a bad wurd. Like fuck. Bit that's a lie. She thinks she knows everything bit she disnie. Bad boays ca'ed me a 'daftie' in a 'spaso' when ah wis in Tesco buyin ma Crunchies. Ah love ma Crunchies. Ah said 'whit's a spaso, Maxine?' She said 'a spastic' Ah said 'whit's a spastic?' She said 'awe shut up, nivir mind' They boays didnie go tae jail. So it's a lie whit Maxine says. In ah'll no shut up.

Ma Mammy says 'dont shout back'. How come? Ah shout back. Ah say 'you ur a spaso' in a say 'fuck' tae.

A big boay battured me. He dragged me up a close in pullt ma troosers doon, bit he coodnie git thim aff because they widnie go ower ma big, big trainers. Ma Daddy says 'if boays try tae touch yer troosers, kick thim in the goollies'. Ma Daddy showed me where goollies ur. So ah kicked the big boay in his goolies in he shoutid 'ya spaso bastard'. That's anither bad wurd. Bit he wis greetin in he ran away.

Ah like that name – 'Spaso' – 'Spaso McPherson' Spaso is like Superman or Spiderman. Ahm gonnie caw masel Spaso McPherson. Ah laughed, in laughed when the big boay ran away. Ah toal Maxine. She didnae laugh. She said ah should huv run away cause ah could huv got raped. How come? Whit's raped? Naebiddy will tell me. Ma Daddy said 'Get tae your bed in stoap askin silly questions.' How come?

See Mellisa it the day centre she hisnie goat tracky boatums in big, big trainers. She's got a luvely blue dress in shoes thit are high up. How come? Her mammy disnie go tae the same shoap is mine in Maxine's. Ah wish ma Mammy wid go tae her shoap. Mellisa looks nice, like the wumman in the chemist. Look it me – Ah'm a big, big fatty, wae big, big trainers in wee, wee troosers. Bit ah um Spaso McPherson.

Spaso On The Bus

Grace Cleary

Naebiddy likes me. How come? When a go oan the bus everybiddy looks up tae the sky, or oot the windae or doon it the flerr. Ah shout 'hullo aw yous'.

The driver says 'move up the bus'. How come? Ah jist say hullo. Ah say 'hullo Mr Driver, gonnie gies a kiss' Ah like kisses. Ma Daddy gies me kisses when he's no mad. The driver says 'dont start'.

Ah sit doon aside any boay oan the bus in a say 'budge up.' Ah say 'Hiv you got a girlfriend?' Bit then they ayweys go tae anither seat. Ah'm no smelly. Ah hid a bath. Why dae they no wahnt tae speak tae me? How come?

They aw talk tae ma Mammy. They doan't even look it me. Ah'm nice tae folk.

Ah ayweys talk tae them. Ah said to Mrs Howie 'Hullo, your herr's nice. Is it a wig?' She walked away. How come? Inna said tae Mrs Marshall 'Hullo, your a big wumman. Ah like yer dress. Ah saw it in the Charity shoap.' She walked away tae, wae a big rid face. Charity shoaps ur smelly. They aw small the same. How come?

Mibbe ah'm invisible. Like Harry Potter when he pits oan that coat in then naebuddy kin see him. Bit ah'm no. Cause when a look doon ah kin see ma big, big trainers. So ah'm still here.

Ah wisht ah wis Harry Potter. He's goat two best pals. Ah've fell oot wae Maxine. She wis ma best pal. She thinks she knows everything bit she disnae. In big Martin says he's no ma boayfriend any mair. He says he loves Melissa. How come? Ah hate Melissa. Ma Mammy says a cannie be Harry Potter, ah kin oanly be me. Bit ah doan't wahnt tae be me cause naebuddy likes me.

Mrs Adams said a wis a croass. How come? Whit's she talkin' aboot? She said tae ma Mammy 'Mrs McPherson Clare is your cross. We all have crosses to bear'.

Ah'm no a cross in am no a bear either. She disnae like me. Ah don't care. In a don't care aboot the folk oan the bus either. Ah jist shout oot bad wurds. Ah say 'bastard' in 'fuck' in then they awe stoap lookin oot the windaes. Ah know they don't like me cause thir mooths ur aw screwed up. Ah jist pit ma tongue oot. Some folk laugh bit some dinnie. How come?

Mrs Forbes wis oan the bus in she telt ma Mammy. Ma Mammy says 'you ur gein me a showin up. Ah'll need tae take ye tae the doctors again' Ah hate the doctors. Last time he gave me wee pink pills thit made dizzy in faw asleep aw the time. Ah flung them doon the lavvy pan. Ma Mammy didnie know. Ah could jist pit ma haun ower ma mooth tae stoap me swearin oan the bus. Bit ma Mammy took me tae see the Doctor. She wanted mair pink pills. He jist talked tae ma Mammy tae. He never even lookt it me. Ma trainers wir still there so a wisnae invisible. The doctor said 'Clare's swearing is in-approp-er--rat. She may have a condition called tooralooralets. We will have to send her off to be assassed'. The doacturs heid went up in doon in, in up in doon in he took ma Mammy's haun. In she wis greetin. How come?

Skellig Michael

Michael Sharp

A flagellum of rock
In a whiplash of salt.
The whetstone of piety
Heavened from hell.

A calice of islands
In a ring of sharks.
Cockstranglingly cold,
Whale deep, carnal.

A *skellig* of monks
With ravaged feet.
The tireless slog
Of shoeless men.

The only way I can express love is by making up some alternative chapter headings for W. G. Sebald's *Rings of Saturn*

Andrew F Giles

I   Francis Bacon, Henry Moore & the third nipple – Mysterious ancestor – 'Oxford & pies': when language coincides – Luck versus fate – The well in the hill – Ring of bright water (Maxwell/ Raine) – Otter Ale – Putting it down – How to say goodbye: shake hands, hug or kiss? – First hard-on – Red sky as seen from the train! – Mindless – The heart under the sea

II   Bloomsbury – Or Euston (depending) – Cards: three face down, three face up – Charles Dickens & the clown – The squirrel – Iris, the fucking French art student – C'est important to leave – Further hard-ons in *le crypte* – Death: coming soon! – The rejection of everything except you – Mysterious ancestor, second part – The sea enters the city

III Playing cards & drinking liquor – My ancestor – Bodies, locked – A heightening of being, remembered – Laughter – *Camusfearna* – Brightness – Saturnine rings of water (London to Bristol) – Forests of street lamps – The sea touches the horizon – Marks, traces, marks

Whales of Iceland

Colin Herd

This is getting to you
from the ocean.
It's really wishy washy
but worldly all the same.
One minute it's coming,
the next it's going.
You never know where you are.

The ocean's like punk, you
have to pretend to be a moron.
It's not as anti-commodification
as everyone seems to think.

One thing about the ocean
is the way sheer magnitude
gets compounded. People say
it's Proustian but I see it more
as a telephone wire wrapped
around a flinty rib that we're stuck
on, getting gnawed to smithereens.
I suppose it is a little Proustian
in that particular sense, like:

somebody save us
from another novel
about a wet young artist
finding his way

and the next moment
the billowing stupor
dissipates: you're twenty
thousand pages in, head
as blank as cheques,
watermarks intact.

I think I have an idea
of the ocean
in which it's really swell
but I know that's severely
outdated and somewhere
between the third and fourth
books in the series the ocean
forgot its manners.

Maybe that's why the lobster blushed.

A good thing about the ocean is
that seapunk never happened here.
Microcultures take longer to rev up.

Must be the salt, in the water. It melts
things and simultaneously grinds them
down, a double cornet of passive
aggressive and aggressive aggressive.

With sprinkles and a flake.

The ocean is an abattoir. Somebody
needs to do something about the ocean
floor.

I don't know, never heard of a mop?

The ocean read Proust but didn't take
much of it in.

If the ocean had a favourite flavour of
ice cream it would be unpalatable
to human tastes.

The ocean doesn't get drunk.

Do you know there's a personal finance
company called Ocean Finance?
They specialise in debt
consolidation, with a sideline
in aggressive advertising.

And do you know what lives
in the ocean?

The opposite of whales.

The Last Pictish Kings

Ian McDonough

Edinburgh, a day before Good Friday,
sunny, kind of cold, the airwaves
talking nothing but elections.
At the pumps the price of petrol
has gone up again:
someone in Falkirk
was bitten by a dog. Kevin's baby
is three months old and thriving.

A second moon of Earth has been detected,
weaving a horseshoe orbit
770 years long. Brora Rangers
have won the Highland League.
My sleep pattern is improving
since I dispensed with bigger pillows.

Our second moon, called Cruithne,
has actually been known since 1986.
Somehow it passed me by.
Recently, discarded
needles litter up the street.
Fashionable cooks are now
deploying coconut oil.
Good for your hair and feet. We are all
poorer without each other.

Edinburgh's Southside is being colonized
by the University. Yesterday
I drank a lot of gin. Shares in tin mining
continue to fluctuate. Beth has a job
in a geological survey, but still
remains addicted to crisps.

The old guys who once would meet
to take a half and half in Southside bars,
like the last Pictish Kings,
feel a rumble underground.
shaking the soles of their feet.

Blow Off

AJ Taudevin

walking one

There's a person.

She's a woman.

She's walking up a street.

You know it. The street.

You've walked up it a hundred times before. You know the one.

With the pharmacy on the corner and the sandwich shop next to that. Come on, you know it. It's got a bank at the start of the pedestrian bit. And the phone shop next that. And the countless clothing outlets that have rows

and rows

and rows

and rows

and rows

and rows of clothes that all look vaguely the same.

You know the street.

It's the one with the chrome benches along the pavement.

Or are they wooden?

Or fake marble?

With the little flower pots around the street lamps.

Or little mini trees.

Demi trees.

Quasi trees.

Don't-grow-any-higher-than-the-first-floor-of-the-Mac-Store-trees.

And the rubbish bin that no matter what seems to always catch on fire filling your airways with the clutch of burning plastic. With the pebbled rings of oblong squished chewing gum encircling it as it snorts toxic smoke into the early morning air.

That street. You know it.

The one that if you look up to above the shop fronts to the tops of the buildings and squint your eyes a bit you could fool yourself into thinking you were walking up that street in the 80's. The 60's. The 40's. 20's. 1916. 1903. 18 hundred and...

That one.

The one that if you look up a bit higher than that and stop squinting your eyes, you can see the clashing glint of the office blocks rising up behind it.

Silver.

Chrome.

Grey.

Glass.

And beyond them again the biggest tower of them all. Rising up out of the pillars of business. Up above them all. A gigantic green, blue, purple shaft. Throbbing as its energy pulses through its electrical veins. Erect and alert.

That office block. That monument to progress. To capital. That shaft. You know the one I'm talking about.

Glinting in the daylight. The streetlight. The early, early, early morning street light. The street. The one that you know. That street.

The street that person is walking up.

That woman.

She's walking alone. No one else is around. But even if they were, if you were there, right now as she walks, you wouldn't notice her. She has mastered the art of walking without you seeing her. Invisible.

Not because she's shy.

Or frightened.

Or abused.

Or homeless.

Or thinks herself ugly.

Or of no value.

But because she has one intention only. To get somewhere. And to not be seen along the way.

And so, I'm not going to tell you what she looks like. Because you wouldn't notice her. So you wouldn't know.

I'm not going to tell you her hair colour.

Her skin colour.

Whether she's got an almond or a heart shaped face.

I'm not going to tell you if she's thin, if she's muscular, curvy, big boned.

I'm not going to tell you what she's wearing. A hoodie. A mini skirt. Combats. Kitten heels. Heavy boots.

I'm not going to tell you if she's wearing a ring on her finger.

Or if she has a boyfriend. Or a girlfriend. Or if she's ever had someone she would call either.

I'm not going to tell you if she has a child. Or once had one. Or was going to have one. And then didn't.

I'm not going to tell you where she was born. Where she went to school. Where she lives now.

I'm not going to tell you her family name. I'm not going to tell you her first name. Or her middle name. Or the names she prefers to go by.

I'm not going to tell you any of this. Not yet. Not yet.

All you need to know, right now. Is that she is a person. Walking up that street, the street that you know, that we all know, on her own, with no one else around, at 3:27 am on a Monday morning, towards that giant glistening tower. That giant glistening shaft. The shaft that you know. That we all know.

With five pounds of dynamite in her bra.

5 4 3 2 1

BLOW OFF

Not yet. Blow off. Not yet.

The Auld Craws

Donald Adamson

frae the Finnish o Lauri Pohjanpää

Aside a loanin twae auld craws
hud perched. They passed the time o day,
nae need o haste, as back-end rain
fell on broun reeds. The lift wis grey.

The oors gaed by. Hauf tae himsel
yin said, 'Ah see the cranes hae flowen.'
Mair silence. Then the ither croaked
'Aye, richt eneuch, the cranes are gane.'

The rain wis drummin on the loch
and yince again the craws wir quate.
Yin rubbed a neb alang his wing,
the ither screwed his een and sat.

A wee bit stink cam frae the byre,
the rain poored doon, and noo the daurk
wis faain ower the furrit field
as baith birds hunched a feathery neck.

Thus on a fence, bedraigelt, wat
the auld craws pondered, deep in thocht,
till wings wir stieve tae stretch and spreid.
'Ah'd best be on ma wey,' yin said.
His frien said, 'Maun, in this braw weather
it's grand tae sit awhile and blether.'

Contributors

Kate Tough

a former assistant professor alumni fellow
his poems appear in the current
his lobster have even crossed the Atlantic

poet, artist, editor, author
former editor of author of co-founder and
recent finalist in a participant
previously taught at later this year
will be upcoming in commissioned and
lives in an award winning *Filling Station*

poems have recently appeared in the 17th-century
poems have appeared in *Waterways* and *Permafrost*

a sixth generation candidate of found poems
has been accepted by various, among others
has been awarded penknives
from the Northwest Cultural College

poetry reader
leader, among others
a few dozen other—
whose names he can't remember offhand

regularly gripes in the Cultural Quarter of Bristol, England
and throughout the United States

in his spare time he likes his sons and wife
(whose names he can't remember offhand)
and writes a daily poem using *The Sow's Ear*
earned a new work grant
to write a new collection of glam rock
it will be named after a racecar driver
fleeting moments can be found here

a writer from the state of *Fragile Context*
she has been told her work is like
caring for potted cacti in Tupelo, Kentucky

she holds degrees in typewriter ribbons and felt-tip pens
her most recent body of work focuses on hardship—
Thrush in its many forms
Thrush in the *Inner Passage*

she finds herself deeply inspired by *The Aquarium*
in which her childhood was steeped

among others and others and other places was born
embracing, questioning and sometimes subverting
often wishes she was a bat

a two-time poet and regulatory compliance supervisor
she ended up in *Badlands* drinking a coke
before deciding to move *Into The Heartland*
now lives in the New York Times crossword puzzle
and elsewhere, both online and in the Hebrides

graduated from pre-kindergarten
received a special mention

a writer from the state of *madeupmovement*
please visit
or follow him

The New Poet
has been writing for many years.

Source: *The Found Poetry Review,* Volume Seven, "Contributors" section.

A Good Life

A Good Cause
Tessa Ransford

Luath Press Ltd., RRP £7.99, 108 pp

Founder of the Scottish Poetry Library, political activist, translator and tireless campaigner for human rights, Tessa Ransford used poetry to make a "better nation". The *Good Cause* of her title resonates throughout this work and her life.

The eponymous first poem cites Thomas Muir's vision for a more just society, "the cause of the People", where the poet chooses Calton Hill over Parnassus, "as Burns would". Ransford asks, "Will it finally prevail?" Her answer is cautionary: "Not while the New Town still / lays its upholstered values / on our systems". This anti-materialist thread binds the collection together, weaving political considerations and a sense of justice with the search for a Scottish identity.

'Cliffs' conveys frustration over the inability to reach a higher truth amidst shallow, transient trends: "...we gather crumbs dropped / from the functional picnics of arts administrators", but the poem ends with a steadfast belief in "a good cause":

> "...we eat our crumb and continue
> our path...
>   our daft but intense belief in our task
> we reach those dunes, those cliffs
> over the sea".

For a woman of many accolades and prestigious awards, the poetry remains grounded:

> "It is hard work –
> from hand to mouth and mouth
> to hand from heart to head
> and head to foot"

Ransford's political activism and environmentalism also ring true. 'The Floating Iceberg's Song' is based on a "news report of an iceberg the size of Hong Kong floating past the African coast":

> "my waters will flow as judgement
> a mighty stream in the desert. [...]
> the planet floats like the Titanic in
> space
>   and can sink, can be utterly
> wrecked".

In 'To remember or not', Ransford recalls the war years. "Memorial events and religiousness I do not enjoy", she says, adding: "...How can I forget the nuclear weapons that lie / behind the lie in acts of official mourning?" Her father is remembered as "he who had 'served' as a sapper and RE signals' officer/ throughout those four insanely slaughterous years"; whilst also recalling him as a "graceful dancer and witty charmer".

The poems move confidently from wider themes to intimate portraits, as Ransford pays tribute to such literary and poetic luminaries as Duncan Glen, Hugh MacDiarmid and Iain Crichton Smith, among others. 'The Great Tapestry of

Scotland: a missing panel' celebrates the Scottish Poetry Library, its logo "a cross-stitched heart" that can be read "in all languages" and uses Iain Crichton Smith's phrase, "the grace that musicks us" to sum up the spirit of this unique institution. Ransford's 'Tribute to Duncan Glen' tells of the man whose design saved the Scottish Poetry Library: *"the brain in your head* made thoughts into words / and sent you for treasure to library hoards". It references a quote from Glen: "If you are born with a love of books and have a brain in your head, I think you just do it".

Despite the knowledge of her impending death, Ransford's writing is clear and controlled, removing herself as subject. In 'The Loving Spirit', the poet is referred to in the third person, or through dialogue: "'I want to die but I don't know how / and her fingers pluck and cling'". 'Endings', the last poem of the collection, uses a "Teddy" with its torn nose and sagging stuffing as a symbol of herself:

> "I've thrown him away
> today [...]
> for he cannot look forward
> to dying"

The collection is dedicated to Dara, her youngest grandchild, and she writes lyrically of her grandchildren, without being overly sentimental. 'Lily of Raasay' ends with a look to the future:

> "Now I behold you
> give you my words.
> When I have left here

> they will be with you
> silently singing
> for all my sweet loves."

– Seawolf

Open Borders

Dacre's War
Rosemary Goring

Polygon, RRP £14.99, 352pp

Dacre's War, Rosemary Goring's follow up to *After Flodden,* remains with the Crozier clan in the Scottish Borders of the sixteenth century and expands scope to include the courts and taverns of France and London. When you're dealing with one of the most treacherous periods of Scottish history, it's a very lucky character that survives from one book to the next. In the ten years between volumes, Adam Crozier has gone some way towards consolidating his power in Teviotdale. With the boy King James V on the throne, a French regent, the Dowager Queen and her husband all tugging at the fabric of state, Scotland is torn into rags. The area is held in pressurized containment by the Warden General, Thomas Dacre. Pitting clans against each other, encouraging lawlessness so the rewards flow into his pockets, Dacre is an old man, tiring of the weather and the daily grind of being Henry VIII's man in the North. He begs the king to let him leave his post, a favour Henry isn't keen to grant. Meanwhile Adam Crozier plots Dacre's downfall in revenge for his father's murder.

Where *After Flodden* echoed with horses' hooves on the rough roads, *Dacre's War* is more of a suspense thriller, full of back room negotiations, court room set-pieces and political intrigue. It's a study in the corruption of power. The long knives are out and the border rings to the tune of vengeance. Behind every damask and tapestry there is a hostile ear.

It's a rollicking good adventure, skilfully plotted by Goring. While Crozier struggles to unite the Borders against Dacre, there are numerous sub-plots and side-games that surpass entertainment. The 'heresy' of the new Protestantism slips in through the character of a French deserter from the Regent's army, while gender politics and social expectations are probed through Adam and Louise's marital tensions. This is an ambitious book with clear, deep knowledge behind it and rewards multiple readings. Academic weight combines with a campfire storyteller's glee to form a welcome addition to the canon of Scottish historical fiction, a genre otherwise dogged by a 'kings-and-claymores' or 'kilts-and-heather' image problem and the perception – rightly or wrongly – that many have taken liberties with their scholarship. From Tom Devine's justifiable labelling of John Prebble's work as 'faction' to the long, dark curse of emotional manipulation *Braveheart* cast over the whole enterprise, our history hasn't always been well served. Yet a recent resurgence, uncoincidentally

arising with the debates around Scottish independence, is giving Scottish historical fiction a new, respectable lease of life. At the forefront is Goring's work and Rona Munro's stunning *James* trilogy, produced by our National Theatre in 2014.

History, as much as art, is the process by which we explore ourselves and craft the narratives that give our nation shape and drive. Post-referendum, while a number of our speculative writers are beginning to explore *what-might-have-been* utopias and *we've-only-ourselves-to-blame* dystopias, a serious, objective reappraisal of our past is also underway that embraces this ambivalence. It's no surprise that Goring's series (there's a strong hint that the story of the Croziers isn't over) is set in the Borders. With its geographical ambiguity and divided loyalties, it's the perfect backdrop for some national self-appraisal. There's none of the Royal Mile gift shop in works like *Dacre's War,* nor is there a mass grave of slaughtered facts. Goring has stripped away history's sepia-tinged distance, its sickly romance and self-pitying tragedy to show us a Scotland coming to terms with its contradictions, picking itself up and dusting itself down. *Dacre's War* contributes an important piece to the next stage of that project.

– *Totoro*

La Peste of times...

Death is a Welcome Guest
Louise Welsh

John Murray, RRP £14.99, 374pp

With the first in the *Plague Times* trilogy, *A Lovely Way to Burn*, Louise Welsh wove the twists and turns of a detective thriller into the dystopian nightmare of a global pandemic. In crumbling post-infection London, the memorable Stevie Flint sought justice for her boyfriend's murder and proved a worthy hero for Welsh's new genre hybrid: apocalypse noir, if you will.

Death is a Welcome Guest returns to London and rewinds to just a few days before "the sweats". Our new protagonist is Magnus McFall, an up-and-coming comedian in a world about to lose its sense of humour. The night before his first big support slot, a drunken act of heroism lands him in prison, locked up with violent criminals as guards and inmates alike succumb to the disease. Magnus emerges to a country transformed by the virus. In the quest to get back to his family in Orkney he falls in with a group of survivors holed up in a country house. Their leaders see the virus as an Old Testament-style purge, a chance for a fresh start, however while they are immune to the bug Magnus finds they are not immune to homicide. When he finds himself investigating a murder, we slowly realise Louise Welsh has once again seeded a much-loved crime scenario inside her post-pandemic hell. There's no sleuth, no butler to cast suspicions on, but

Welcome Guest is in many respects a big-house murder mystery.

The *Plague Times* novels pose an interesting dilemma. Crime fiction is celebrated for providing a perverse comfort: detective restores order, exorcises death. But who cares to solve a murder when death has already taken the majority? In a time of plague, life becomes either very valuable or very cheap. While a sense of justice may be all anyone has left to keep them going, Death is not so much the guest at this party, he's the host.

Given the publication dates, this episode, in particular, might one day be read as Welsh's commentary on indyref. It begins in a London rotting with literal corruption; it is Scotland Magnus looks to with hope. While the survivors he meets beyond the capital are a diverse bunch, their utopian pitch sounds distinctly conservative. Despite his pull to the North, the rest of the community insist that Magnus must stay, that they will be better together and Union flags make a potent appearance at the novel's climax.

Yet, the novel's primary source material is not recent British politics, but history. The author commands a historian's eye for the sociology of mass-mortality, ultimately posing the question: which is the worse horror, to perish in a holocaust or to survive it? Welsh has already named as her inspiration the nightmare visions of a Cold War childhood: the BBC classics, *Survivors* and *Threads*. Such thought-experiments in catastrophe let writers take society apart to see what makes it tick. The horror is in the truth of what we find out.

As the grim shade of animosity between old superpowers haunts us once again, we realise those bad dreams never went away.

– *Shadowfax*

Knowledge, which You don't have Yet

Fios
Stewart Sanderson

Tapsalteerie, RRP £5.00, 39pp

I'm always suspicious of back cover notes that insist a book "marks the emergence of an important new voice" aware that the poets' friends are often invited to write the same or a publisher, with an eye to sales. Fair enough. On this occasion, however, I must agree.

Edwin Morgan Poetry Award shortlisted, Stewart Sanderson's sensational debut pamphlet *Fios* (pronounced 'fiss' I learn) not only offers the promise of a major new Scottish voice, but one that, although rooted in his devotion to the Scots language and landscape, has something to say we all might want to hear.

Sanderson's work demands you visit or revisit works of art, amateur black and white film footage or recall the dimly remembered history of a revolutionary poet, because only by doing so can we can plug into the *'fios'* – "knowledge, which you don't have yet" (from 'Fios', appropriately the first poem in the collection) – which Sanderson's work, on careful examination, gives up.

Poetry tells you things you know but do not know you know, shines light into the dark corners of things, offers a sense of something better understood. It peals back sensibilities in the same way Sanderson's fine poem 'Tradition Bearer' peals back centuries from the moment his downstairs neighbour pushes a "pound note" under his infant pillow so he should "dae right" to...

"a very ancient man
with a face like teak
a voice the colour of smoke
(who) said when *he* was four
he could mind the boy riding
white-faced through the village, shouting
Culloden was lost."

Not only does Sanderson perfectly articulate a sense of belonging in our own histories but, as other poems show, a sense of belonging in the Scots language as well. Yes, I had to Google words from old Scots, words like "crotal" (sheep bells), "waulking songs" (songs sung by women beating tweed to soften it), "smirr" (drizzly rain) and "cladach" (beach or shore), but these may be better known to some Scots readers and their discovery and the richness of their sounds added a fresh dimension to my own joy in the work. Listen to the onomatopoeia he seizes from the use of "cladach" in 'Botticelli's Illustration for Purgatorio 11' for instance: "the calm cladach / where sea-sick spirits wretch.", shore just wouldn't have done it.

And yes, I did need to reacquaint myself with those paintings and histories, for at twenty-five, Sanderson is very wise and mightily well-informed. But then he rewards research a hundred-fold by offering new perspectives or exploding the expectations of early iconographic interpretations, as in 'Portrait of a Young Married Couple' inspired by Jan Van Eyck's famous painting..

> "That terrier we see
> between the lovers' legs would sooner steal
> a chop than symbolise their hearts' desires."

No Renaissance symbol of marital fidelity and love there, then? Here is a poet who writes of love with a lyrical simplicity as in 'Early Afternoon in America', "I miss your tenement / where sleep grows, / softer than some rare / beast's fur" but who also retains a deep understanding of the craft of poetry, has the measure of free verse in his bones and, it seems, the invisible scaffolding of more formal structures at his beck and call.

This is a small book of big ideas by a poet who will no doubt confirm in time the self-fulfilling prophesy on the back cover.

– *Macavity*

The Outsider in Wester Ross

His Bloody Project
Graeme Macrae Burnet

Contraband, RRP £8.99, 278pp

His Bloody Project is Graeme Macrae Burnet's second novel and like his first, *The Disappearance of Adèle Bedeau*, a literary thriller. Whereas *Disappearance* was indebted to the European crime novels of the mid-20th century, and especially those by Georges Simenon, on whom Burnet is something of an expert, this more recent book resembles Margaret Atwood's *Alias Grace* (1996) inasmuch as it is set in the middle of the 19th century, in an unforgiving landscape and turns on the question of a murderer's guilt.

If Atwood's novel conjured a vivid and thoroughly convincing picture of Canada in 1843, Burnet's does the same for a Wester Ross crofting community in 1869, recounting a triple murder in the village of Culduie, south of Applecross. The novel is assembled from statements given to police by the residents of Culduie, an "Account" by the murderer himself, Roddy Macrae, the memoirs of a vainglorious 'expert' in criminal anthropology, a report of the trial compiled "from contemporary newspaper coverage and the volume *A Complete Report of the Trial of Roderick John Macrae published by William Kay of*

Edinburgh 1869." In collating a number of conflicting versions of the same events, genuine doubt is planted in the reader's mind as to Roddy's guilt in a manner not dissimilar to Alasdair Gray's great 1992 novel *Poor Things*. And, like Gray, Burnet claims to have simply "edited and introduced" the documents that make up his novel.

While *His Bloody Project* is rooted, like *Poor Things*, in Scotland and its history, Burnet brings to his novel a more continental appreciation of crime fiction's potential existentialism. Roddy displays a disregard for the consequences of his actions, repeatedly states that he has "no intention" of denying responsibility for his crimes and offers no resistance to his arrest for three murders. He only pleads not guilty by reason of insanity to please his advocate, Sinclair, who spies an opportunity to advance his career in a trial that has captured the public's imagination. There is something here of Camus' Meursault in Roddy's indifference.

While the novel utilizes different voices to tell the story, they are similar in style. All describe human behaviour – both the rational and the *ir*rational – in a matter-of-fact way, pared down to paratactic precision. This droll delivery allows for sly humour and Burnet wisely understands that less is often more, as in Roddy's description of his intoxication at a summer gathering: "In order to express my high spirits, I climbed onto a table and poured a tankard of ale over my head". Understatement is deployed again,

to shocking effect, in the novel's account of the brutal murders. An unadorned style is also well-suited to depicting the crofters' existence. Roddy's account in particular pays close attention to everyday objects and material activities: their carbohydrate-intensive diet, the textures of the landscape, the drudgery of work.

The novel's lack of indulgence or superfluity echoes the Presbyterian outlook of Roddy's father, who exhibits an acceptance of his fate (what he calls "the powers-that-be") that is not a million miles away from an existentialist's. Burnet skilfully marshals his 'sources' so as to not disappoint the reader; it is to his great credit that the novel's central question is never fully answered.

– Mr Mistoffelees

Granite of the Soul

Nae Floors
Ann McKinnon

Tapsalteerie, RRP £5.00, 31 pp

Stones, structures, communities and things that are, or could be, solid; Ann McKinnon's collection grounds the reader to these fundamental elements to preserve the granite/smeddum of the Scots. It is stories and the telling of them within family and community that keep this metanarrative alive, as in the fireside "craic" in 'Chaff', for example:

> "We hunker roon the brace,
> they'd get a blaze
> gawn in the hearth an craic aboot
> work."

And yet, places, language and memories are shaded in a deep-wrung regret for the loss that time brings, such as the way The Mistress Stane of St Kilda "lowers ower us / Fu o fulmars and their bairns." In 'Fulmars' Land – St Kilda' only birds remain, "The folk hid tae gan awa" and "stane dykes run intae naithin."

However, in 'Fund a Faimilie on Muck' where the narrator is "Seekin Kin" on the isle of Muck, there's less romantic nostalgia and more a clear recognition of the impact of poverty and hardship.

> "we stravaiged aboot,
> taken in the dreichness
> fell gled oor kin had lowped awa.
> They spend aw thir time in the fields
> rakin
> a raw livin fae saund and barren
> stane"

In the end it's their own "kin" that keeps them going, keeps "them fae takin a scunner." Even when the mud "is slurpin, squelchin" or when "the rain is beatin doon", the sun can shudder "intae view", "mindin me o why I'm here, / comin haim tae ye" as in the case of 'The Walk'. Through all, the language must hold; there is a determination, a "gowpin" for "the words o ma bairnhood" to aid the poet's

"screivin at stanes."

This makes for a deeply personal collection. McKinnon's father; the "Staunin Stane", "aye minded" her about the "wirds". And she writes of a gathering when "it wis John wha insisted / We spak the gather in Scots." In 'The Grundstane', McKinnon invites the reader to celebrate the tenacity of these men, to "fill up a tassie / And drink tae John / The grundstane to aw oor craic." Memories of place, people – the structures and ties that bind – abound in Ann McKinnon's writing: warm and embracing, heartfelt and sad.

'Mindings' perfectly captures those moments when we take comfort in those "jewels...in the pooch" of the mind. Here, we "Mind the time", remember "...yon nicht" and "whit aboot when"; running with the narrator to identify the ways by which we go "seekin solace" in times of loss. The regret that 'Nae Floors' were taken to the headland cemetery is offset by the wild "yella clump, grippin the dry stane", the "richt wraith." Here, in this titular poem, there is a resolute resilience that will overcome the "daurkness" or "tears in the murkiness".

Reminiscent of MacCaig, 'The Lichthoose' is painted there for the reader to see and is a solid metaphor, a guarantee that "the licht aye comes agin."

– Baxter's Old Ram

For the Love of Science

The Need for Better Regulation of Outer-Space: A Collection of Stories
Pippa Goldschmidt

Freight, RRP £8.99, 178 pp

Fiction about science is unfortunately a much rarer beast than science fiction. Since C P Snow wrote about the British nuclear bomb project in the latter half of the 1940s, few authors have operated so clearly and expressively in this field than Goldschmidt.

Her well-crafted stories move from the mundane, all too smelly world of the laboratory to larger geo-political, environmental, sexual-political and historical concerns. Her characters are generally scientists, or of that milieu, living what are occasionally sterile, middle-class lives, as if the content and methodology of science renders them brittle and almost without breath. Intriguingly, Goldschmidt's crisp and engaging prose uncovers deep humanity, compassion and genuine tenderness, for example Alan Turing's discovery in 'The Snow White Paradox',

"There. Breasts. He has breasts, small but decidedly feminine in shape. This is what they've done to him. There was a man in ancient times called Tiresias, Alan learnt about him at school. He

was also a paradox, he was a man with breasts, and he was a blind man who could see."

While the genius of the scientific method and of what it has given humanity is not to be ignored, the central paradox of the nuclear bomb undercuts many claims science might have to morality. As Glasgwegian poet Thomas Campbell wrote in 1799 "O star-eyed Science! hast thou wandered there, / To waft us home the message of despair?"

This theme is best explored in the excellent and fascinating 'Heroes and Cowards': a fictionalised account of Bertolt Brecht's time in exile in the USA working with actor Charles Laughton on the play 'The Life of Galileo'. In a parallel narrative it is revealed that both Brecht and Robert – Daddy of the Bomb – Oppenheimer are being spied upon by agents from The House Un-American Activities Committee (HUAC). The poignant irony that a committee set-up in 1938 to act as a bulwark against Nazism is by 1946 investigating one of the world's most famous anti-Nazi campaigners on suspicion of Communist sympathies is deliciously rendered and belies the scale of the US ruling elite's paranoia. Charles Laughton is beautifully depicted here and, as in the earlier 'The Snow White paradox' featuring Alan Turing, there is intense sympathy for the predicament of gay men at a time of great sexual hypocrisy. For both Brecht and Oppenheimer there are many parallels to be drawn between their lives and works. Both are new Galileos challenging authority, but each by different means. Laughton is an outsider who has found a kind of 'English' compromise that allows him to live almost contentedly in the Hollywood hills, but the HUAC spies are always lurking. Every character appears compromised by the historical moment of their existence, including the spy from whose viewpoint much of the story is told,

"I should be out there, working, gathering information. But after I'd had to translate some of Brecht's poetry for the hearing I'd got into the habit of reading it. I pick up my notebook and thumb through it until I reach the poem that keeps singing in my head:

Just whose city is the city?
Just whose world is the world?"

These short stories provide a highly original, and engagingly human, slant on science and its practitioners past and present. Read and enjoy.

– *Towser*

Caledonia Homesick Blues

Sputnik Caledonia
Andrew Crumey

Dedalus, RRP £9.99, 553 pp

Parallel worlds, or the Multiverse theory, feature prominently in recent Scottish writing. The best known examples are Alasdair Gray's *Lanark* and Iain Banks' *The Bridge*, two books where real life runs parallel to another, more fantastic, although often dystopian world, with the central character inhabiting both. Andrew Crumey's *Sputnik Caledonia* is another example to add to the list. Set initially in a recognisable 20th century Scotland, Robbie Coyle's story also takes place in a military-controlled fantasy future. The past is cloaked in nostalgia for an ideal and idealised childhood, which most readers will identify with to some degree, while the future examines what pressures come to bear on an individual once that childhood ends. The former is fantasy set in reality, the latter a harsh reality set in a fantastic world, and Crumey uses this device to ask interesting philosophical, political, scientific and moral questions.

It's a structure that initially poses a problem, as Crumey's depiction of Robbie's childhood is so vivid you may be tempted to linger there. The young Robbie is obsessed with space and dreams of becoming a cosmonaut – a particular stance swayed by his fervently socialist father. Crumey sees the world through a child's eyes quite beautifully, inviting long forgotten memories and musings to come to the fore. These include believing your parents are not who they say they are, trying to understand why certain family rules apply only to you, and the confusing approach of lust and attraction from an already uncertain adult world. Robbie struggles to come to terms with his growing up, armed only with his increasingly vivid imagination.

Just as we are getting comfortable in Robbie's childhood, he and we are suddenly thrown into the future. Although jarring at first, you begin to get your bearings when you realise this world is just as involving if much more threatening. It is a society where paranoia rules, something the state openly encourages and supports. Robbie still dreams of going into space and is competing against other candidates to fulfil his ambition. Many tests and tribulations are placed in his way, in all aspects of his life. Sex, for instance, is used as collateral, to blackmail, and sometimes even more bizarrely. Without going into details here, the phrase "I think I saw the Red Star" may be one you use in the future.

It could be read as a warning against the communism that Robbie's father desires, but I don't believe Crumey is being that specific. Rather, this is a warning of how the individual can be controlled and suppressed by any government that professes to act for the greater good, and Robbie finds himself having to break their rules to survive. The comparison with Iain Banks is a particularly apt one as Crumey

not only shares his sense of humour but also his political rigour, and like *The Bridge, Sputnik Caledonia* tests free will against state control.

It is a novel which is as ambitious as the young Robbie Coyle himself, and similarly threatens to fail at times, but when you reach the unexpectedly emotional finale you are in awe that Crumey has, once again, pulled it off. When taken with his other novels *Pfitz* and *The Secret Knowledge,* it could be argued that Andrew Crumey is not only one of the most interesting and challenging novelists around, but one of the very best. He may be your new favourite writer; you just don't know it yet. Universally approved.

– *Kes*

Cruel Waters?

The Jump
Doug Johnstone

Faber & Faber, RRP £12.99, 288 pp

The Jump by Doug Johnstone is a gutsy novel dealing with the aftermath of suicide. When fifteen year old Logan Napier takes his own life by jumping off the notorious Forth Road Bridge, his mum, Ellie, is consumed with guilt and crushed by grief. Obsessed by her son's death, she watches CCTV footage over and over again in a hopeless attempt to understand the final moments of Logan's life. Meanwhile, her husband Ben turns conspiracy theorist in his pained bid to comprehend his only child's death. One night, on a routine pilgrimage to the bridge, Ellie comes across Sam McKenna, a 17 year-old boy attempting to end his life, too. Ellie intervenes, taking Sam home where she discovers a dark secret. Struggling to cope with Logan's death, Ellie projects her sorrow and desperate need for forgiveness onto Sam. Risking everything for a stranger, Ellie entangles herself in the lives of the McKenna family in an impossible cry for redemption.

Writing about suicide is no easy feat and Johnstone is graphic; courageously refusing to shy away from his intimate and gut-wrenching portrayal of those left behind. Nor does he land on a convenient explanation as to why a fifteen-year-old boy might take his own life. Mental illness provides no real answers and with a determined pen Johnstone creatively forbids the living in his book from making sense of Logan's death, though they go to extraordinary lengths to do so. Ellie marks the location of her son's end across her body with tattoos and daringly swims in the precarious waters below the bridge, edging closer to the reasoning that took her son. Ben frantically leaflets and persecutes developers in the area where they live, blaming chemicals from constructive manufacturing for fatally altering his son's state of mind. Ultimately, Ellie and Ben are chasing the impenetrable belief that it was somehow in their power to keep their son alive, when it was only ever in Logan's

power. Presented with the opportunity to save other vulnerable teens, Ellie and Ben find themselves in cruel waters again, seeking salvation for their son's death but running the risk of losing each other. Ben and Ellie come to understand Logan may have died but their love for one another remains strong. The loving parents they once were finally emerge from the icy sea and though they have no child to reflect this, they can always look to each other for what was lost.

Johnstone's depiction of the impact on living after suicide is painfully perceptive, made without judgment or smug ponderings. His openness as a writer provides a relentless read. He bravely and sensitively tackles the subject of mental illness and its repercussions for society, taking us where we are often afraid to go as readers. *The Jump* is an uncompromising page-turner, an unforgettable book possessed of great tragedy and empathy, a truly honest novel that it is impossible to turn away from.

– *Sabina*

Magic For All

The Magicians of Scotland
Ron Butlin

Polygon, RRP £9.99, 109pp

As the title suggests, *The Magicians of Scotland* follows on from Ron Butlin's previous collection, *The Magicians of Edinburgh* which emerged from the poet's first term as Edinburgh Makar (2008-2011). The present volume collects the fruits, commissioned or otherwise, of Butlin's second and final term in office from 2012 to 2014. Divided into three sections, 'Magic Places', 'Magic People' and 'Magic For All', it sees him casting his net a little wider both within and outwith Scotland, for all that the nation's capital remains a key source of subject matter.

As he says himself on his website, Butlin believes that "Laureateship is A Good Thing". There are, admittedly, a few ways of looking at it. In an age where poets sometimes struggle to reach readers not themselves engaged in writing poetry, the desire to reach and be responsible towards a larger community is understandable. On the other hand, the practicalities of such public appointments can be restrictive. Though there have been notable exceptions, few poets write their best work as laureates.

Butlin's best work is very fine indeed. Perhaps it's unfair to compare the Makar poems in *The Magicians of Scotland*, written to some extent in response to official requirements, too directly with others, presumably born of internal necessity. Much of the book would probably work well in performance – indeed, the seven-part sequence 'The Commonwealth Games' was written to be read (guess where) alongside jazz accompaniment. I enjoyed the wordplay of the fourth section, 'India (Raga)', which is made up entirely from Indian place names. Another site-specific sequence, 'Stations of the Rush Hour', can apparently be found on the timetables of Edinburgh's tram stops, with a poem for each station from York Place to the Airport. Puckishly, the one for Princes Street notes that "the budget allowed for one stop only / along the entire length of our capital's main street" and urges passengers to make the most of it.

Elegantly illustrated by James Hutcheson, most of the poems in *The Magicians of Scotland* also carry short prose introductions, glossing the text for readers unfamiliar with Skara Brae and the Ninth Legion, for instance. On the whole, I didn't feel these explanations added much to my experience of the work itself. Though there's nothing wrong with occasional poetry, I don't think it's all that unreasonable to expect poetry to be its own occasion. While notes can help elucidate a difficult poem, in the age of Google it's not so hard for people who don't know what Skara Brae is to find out for themselves. Contemporary laureates are to some extent required to be ambassadors for their art. However, it needn't follow that they do all the work for the reader.

Perhaps unsurprisingly, the poems I found most effective were the more personal where Butlin dispensed with paraphrases, trusting his public to make the extra effort. In the elegiac 'Remembering a Good Friend', Butlin writes, both wittily and movingly

"No history but what we take for granted. Our lives are

as already read. And here's the writing on the wall.

We wrote it."

'All That We Have', which concludes the second section, is a finely held love poem. The last poem in the book, 'Prayer', is similarly strong, ending

> "when I return at last to this same
> hour
> and this same place,
> let there be someone raising even
> the emptiness in their hands
> towards me."

For all the occasional inconsistency of The Magicians of Scotland, lines like these ring true.

– *Crow*

Dear Gutter

I'm tired of being just a girlfriend and want more from my partner but he doesn't feel the same.

I'm a woman in my mid-thirties. I've been in a relationship for five years with a kind, considerate man who I love. I feel the time is right to deepen our commitment to each other. However, despite being someone who's articulate, empathetic and who can talk about his emotions, my partner shows no signs of being interested in taking things to the next level – despite heavy hints. He says he loves me, but actions speak louder than words. Should I issue an ultimatum and risk losing him? It would break my heart for things to end over this but I'm increasingly dissatisfied with the status quo.

Gutter says:

It's always dangerous to generalise about the disparities between men and women but – deep breath – I'm going to here. Regardless of your position on nature versus nurture (personally, I'm with nurture...), to even the most casual of observers there are undeniable differences in male and female attitudes to relationships.

The cultural cliché is the 90s BBC sit-com *Men Behaving Badly* – where two women try to negotiate their respective relationships with two flat-sharing man-boys. The `boys' are laddish at best, boorish at worst, selfish, un-housetrained and child-like. The women aren't – they're women, rather than girls. They want their men to stop behaving like dicks, grow up and settle down. Comedy has always needed grotesques but men must've found this programme excruciating, so appalling was its representation of masculinity of the era. However, stereotypes need a ring of truth to exist.

Today's twenty or thirty-something man may well be more emotionally conversant, but underneath, the same gender differences are reinforced daily by wider culture. Men are required to be strong. Men who talk about emotional problems risk appearing weak, to each other and to their partners. While the female archetype may be coquettish and fertile, the male equivalent is a loner, a potent fixer of problems who rides off into the sunset when his work is done.

Western society teaches girls to analyse motives and emotions in order to achieve consensus and co-operation. Boys use humour to negotiate their natural instincts for competition and hierarchy. We honour women who are `nice' and men who are powerful. When men and women talk about love invariably they're talking about completely different things. The result, to my mind, is that women are often a decade or two ahead of men in emotional maturity. Women see a relationship as a journey towards greater intimacy. Men see it as a destination, a comfy room where they relax. For men, relationships are static, while for women they're dynamic.

So what does the woman who wants greater commitment from her partner do? There are two schools of thought. Both have risks. The first is the shotgun. An ultimatum is stressful, creates emotional conflict, but may force a reluctant or emotionally disengaged man to wise up. Your partner may run a mile but if he doesn't he could resent his loss of freedom further down the line. The alternative approach is to wait, slowly working away at his emotional defences. Fatherhood is one life event that can propel a man into greater emotional maturity. The downsides for you include a lack of deeper fulfilment and an imbalance in the relationship as, along with countless other women, you take sole responsibility for its emotional health. This is a lonely place and can reinforce his behaviours rather than breaking them.

There are no easy answers I'm afraid. The most important thing is to talk with honesty. It can feel like dancing across a minefield but it's something that couples in functioning relationships should do as a matter of course. You may have to help your partner reach emotions that are buried deep. It may take a long time. Ultimately you're the only one who can judge if it'll be worth it.

Contributor Biographies

Patricia Ace published *Fabulous Beast* (Freight Books) in 2013 and is currently working on her second collection.

Juana Adcock is a poet and translator working in English and Spanish. Her first collection, *Manca*, was published in Mexico in 2014.

Donald Adamson's collections include *A Landscape Blossoms Within Me* (Arc) and *Glamourie* (Indigo Dreams).

Robert James Berry lives and writes in Dunedin, New Zealand. His latest collection *Gorgeous* (Sylph Editions) is out soon.

Andrew Blair is a writer/performer and the ex-Godfather of Edinburgh poetry. He helps run a podcast called *Poetry as F*ck*.

William Bonar is a recipient of a New Writers Award. His award winning pamphlet, *Offering*, is available from Red Squirrel Press.

Alistair Braidwood runs the Scottish cultural website *Scots Whay Hae!* and his reviews are found in the more discerning publications

Hazel Buchan Cameron's first full collection comes out with Red Squirrel Press in September. hazelbuchancameron. co.uk

John Burnett has written academic and other material on Scottish culture. He is now trying more experimental styles.

Grace Cleary has written three plays. Her favourite character is the feisty, indomitable Spaso in her short monologues.

Jenni Daiches writes poetry, fiction and, as Jenni Calder, non-fiction. Her novel *Borrowed Time* (Vagabond Voices) is out in June.

RA Davis was born in Edinburgh in 1983. He grew in Kent and North Wales and belongs to Glasgow.

Jim Ferguson lives and writes in Glasgow. Fascinating website: jimferguson poet.co.uk

Georgi Gill is a poet whose work has featured in *Bare Fiction*, *Interpreter's House*, *Far Off Places* and *Dactyl*.

Marjorie Lotfi Gill is Poet in Residence at Jupiter Artland. Her poems have been published in the UK and US, and read on BBC Radio 4.

Colin Herd is a poet and Lecturer in Creative Writing at University of Glasgow.

Dave Hook writes rhymes. Front man of hip-hop group Stanley Odd, his work is finding its way onto the page and the stage.

Andrew F Giles has been widely published in journals and anthologies. He researches poetry and antipsychiatry in Bristol.

Harry Giles is a writer and performer. His latest publication is *Tonguit* (Freight). A full portfolio of works is at harrygiles.org

Linda Jackson is a writer, tutor, literary host and musician. She has published short stories and poems and currently writing novel, *The Mark of the Rose*.

Stuart Johnstone is a City of Literature Trust emerging writer and was shortlisted for the 2016 Guardian Short Story Competition.

Robin Jones has been published in *Jacobin*, *The Huffington Post* and *The Edinburgh Review*.

Leyla Josephine has been writing and performing spoken word for two years. Usually Glasgow-based, she is currently living in Japan.

Judith Kahl is a poet, writer, translator, and many other things. Customers who liked this item also liked: poetickindness. wordpress.com

Rached Khalifa teaches Irish literature. He has published critical articles and books on Yeats and other poets.

Henry King teaches English Literature at Malmö Högskola and sometimes blogs at henrymking.blogspot.com

Marek O Lasce is set and lighting designer and alumnus of Glasgow University.

Martin Law writes novels and short fiction. Martin sometimes likes to have fun with words and pictures, and words and sounds.

Iain Maloney is the author of three novels, *First Time Solo, Silma Hill* and *The Waves Burn Bright*. @iainmaloney

Lynsey May lives, loves and spins stories of all sizes in Edinburgh.

Carl Macdougall is a writer, journalist and broadcaster, and teaches at the University of the West of Scotland.

MacGillivray has eaten broken chandelier glass in Berlin, wolf-walked through the backstreets of Vegas, and done much more besides.

Katharine McMahon is author of *The Crimson Rooms* and the award-winning *Rose of Sebastopol*.

Ian McDonough's latest collection is *A Witch Among the Gooseberrie*, and poems have appeared in *Poetry Review* and *Dark Horse*.

Hugh McMillan's Selected Poems, *Not Actually Being in Dumfries*, have just been published by Luath Press.

Callum McSorley is a graduate of the University of Strathclyde where he studied English, Journalism & Creative Writing.

Nick-e Melville rarely does the right thing.

Wendy Miller is a Glasgow-based writer, theatre maker and poet. She works as a creative writing tutor in HMP Barlinnie.

Aidan Moffat has been making music since 1996. His children's book, *The Lavender Blue Dress*, was published in 2014.

Donald S Murray is from Ness in the Isle of Lewis. Now living in Shetland, his latest book is *Herring Tales* (Bloomsbury).

Jamie Norman has appeared in *Causeway / Cabshair, Abridged, Octavius*, and *The Eildon Tree*. Tweets @normantweets

Lisa O'Donnell has written two books *Closed Doors* and *The Death of Bees*, which won The Commonwealth Book Prize in 2013 and an ALEX Award in 2014.

Nalini Paul's poetry explores landscape and memory. Her collaborations include dance, film and visual art. She is currently working on a project for stage.

Collette Rayner is a visual artist and writer. She has had her work in *HOAX*, Standpoint Futures, and Print Festival Scotland.

Olive M Ritch is an Orcadian poet currently working on the final draft of her book-length sequence of poems: Returns of the Past.

Calum Rodger is a poet, performer and scholar. His pamphlet *Know Yr Stuff: Poems on Hedonism* is published by Tapsalteerie.

Andrew Rubens' collaborative translations with Henry King of Benjamin Fondane's poetry are published by NYRB this year.

Chrys Salt MBE is a poet, performer, AD of The Bakehouse, Galloway and Convener of the BIG LIT Festival.

Stewart Sanderson received an Eric Gregory Award in 2015. His first poetry pamphlet is *Fios* (Tapsalteerie, 2015).

Michael Sharp attended the Royal Conservatoire of Scotland and has a doctorate from the University of Wisconsin-Madison.

AJ Taudevin is an acclaimed playwright and broadcaster based in Glasgow.

ES Thomson's third novel is *Beloved Poison* and was published by Constable in March.

Kate Tough's *Head for the Edge, Keep Walking* (Freight) is out now, and a pamphlet is on the way from Tapsalteerie. katetough.com

Lynnda Wardle received a SBT New Writer's Award (2007) and has been published in *thi wurd* and *New Writing Scotland*. lynndawardle.com

Mark West teaches at Glasgow University, edits *Glasgow Review of Books*, and writes for *3am Magazine*, *Review31*, and *The List*.

Allison Whittenberg is a poet and novelist living in Philadelphia. She is the author of four novels, all from Random House.

Alice S Yousef is a Palestinian writer, poet and translator working towards a first collection. @Aliceyousef